The New World War

A Behind-the-Scenes Look at Why and How Militant Muslims Plan to Destroy Western Civilization

John Clark Mead

xulon
PRESS

Xulon Press
11350 Random Hills Road
Suite 800
Fairfax, VA 22030
(703) 279-6511
XulonPress.com

To order additional copies, call 1-866-909-BOOK (2665).

www.new-world-war.com

Introduction

The biblical account of how Moses sent what might be considered spies into Canaan can be found in the 13th chapter of Numbers. After the Exodus from Egypt, Moses led the tribes of Israel throughout a vast wilderness as the Lord directed their path. Slowly making their way to the Promised Land, they settled for some time at a location within the Desert of Paran. From this encampment, Moses selected twelve leaders and sent them north into Canaan in order to ascertain just what sorts of enemies the Children of Israel would eventually have to face. After forty days, the men returned and gave their report to the whole Israelite community. To the discouragement of many the men shared the fact that Israel would, indeed, have to face awesome enemies.

In a very real way, I know exactly how those twelve men must have felt. I say this because through an extraordinary set of circumstances, taking many years to unfold, I eventually found myself "behind-the-lines" separating those who appreciate western civilization and those actively planning its destruction. Moreover, I had the unique opportunity to witness the seeds of militancy take root among Islamic groups and to have the detailed plans for the destruction of the West patiently explained to me by a dear friend who risked his life in doing so.

The first four chapters of this book outline the journey that gave me access to the information I eventually discovered. They relate how my life was transformed from that of a banker in suburban America to a cultural anthropologist who found himself among 500,000 Muslims gathered at a rally deep within the Islamic world to denounce America with all the hatred they could muster. The section ends with the account of how I watched in horror as an ingenious plan that resulted in the loss of thousands of lives unfolded before my eyes.

In chapters five through seven I address the nature of those who count themselves our mortal enemies and the reasons why they have chosen to wage war against the West. I explain why the opinion that those responsible for the events of September 11, 2001, are only a relatively small group of radical Islamic terrorists represents a very dangerous underestimation of the truth.

In chapters eight through ten the question of how militant Muslims plan to destroy western civilization is answered in detail. I will show how the strategy adopted represents years of patient planning by a small group of brilliant men, and how they have effectively communicated their "blueprint for destruction" to thousands of warriors willing to die to ensure its success. The advantages held by those seeking to implement the plan, as well as several key limitations, are also outlined.

In the concluding chapter encouragement is offered to Americans by suggesting that throughout our history, times of adversity have served to strengthen and unite us in a way that seems impossible in times of peace and prosperity.

It is interesting to note that of the twelve men who explored the land of Canaan, only two, Caleb and Joshua, confidently suggested that Israel should face the enemies they had seen. The other men, realizing the strength of the enemies, made great efforts to dissuade their fellow Israelites from taking such action. As Americans and people of other western nations come to terms with the true character of the enemy facing us today, as they begin to understand the tremendous number of individuals involved in this epic struggle, and as they realize the ingenious nature of the plans that have been drawn up against us, it is my hope that we, as Caleb and Joshua, will place our faith in God, realizing that without Him we could have achieved nothing thus far, and will have no hope of success in the future.

Before closing this introduction, I would like to note that in various places throughout this work I have emphasized the very important point that when I speak of Muslims who count themselves our enemies, I am referring specifically and exclusively to those within the realm of militant Islam who have chosen to target the West for annihilation or subjugation. I am in no way referring to the vast majority of Muslims who seek nothing more than to practice their faith while living at peace with all men. It has been my very great privilege for almost half my life to count many Muslims among my dearest friends. I offer this work for their benefit, as well as for the purpose of informing my fellow citizens of the western world of the very real threat that will undoubtedly become increasingly apparent as the months and years unfold.

Contents

Contents

Chapter One

A Noble Cause

I often wonder to what degree the past influences the present. Are we truly masters of our own destiny, or does that from which we come in some way guide us as we undertake our unique journey from birth to the grave? Even as a child these thoughts gave rise to much contemplation in what I now recognize as a restless mind.

God Calling

My family had lived in New England for some three hundred years by the time I arrived on the scene. Reminders of those who had gone before remain plentiful yet today. Homes, churches, and certainly graves serve as physical reminders of those who walked the same ground as me. For as long as I can remember there have been stories told of those who lived in those homes, led those churches, and then inhabited those graves.

Among my favorite memories as a young boy was having many opportunities to visit with my grandmother. It seemed that no matter what the topic of conversation was, I would always have a way of steering the discussion toward the subject of my great grandfathers who were remembered for their heroic deeds in various wars. On one such occasion my grandmother, suddenly realizing that I was old enough to read, led me to an antique bookcase. Selecting a large volume, she handed it to me and suggested that it was about time I learned for myself about all those men and women who had fascinated me for so long.

And so it was that I held in my hands the fullest possible accounts of those who had become my heroes. With great anticipation I carefully examined each page and photograph. After promising to be extraordinarily careful with this and a few other books I was given permission to take them home.

I quickly discovered that the volumes held far more than I had ever been told. Beginning with French royalty in the 10th century, the records traced our family's ancestry with amazing detail for more than thirty generations as our line moved from France to England and finally in 1656 to Boston. The entries were surprisingly detailed. They included records of births, marriages, deaths, and much of what had taken place between these rights of passage. Accounts of crusaders, soldiers, men of God, educators, and simple farmers were found in the pages of our family's past.

I cannot imagine a young mind being more completely enthralled as mine became while reading about all that had been accomplished across the ages by those who shared my bloodline. And, yet, a sense of responsibility accompanied my excitement. How would I add to my family's honorable lineage? What would my record hold? What would my contribution be when compared to those who preceded me?

More than anything else I wanted my life to count. I wanted to contribute something meaningful to the world, just as so many of my forefathers had done. Yet, each who had made significant contributions seemed to have a passion for some great cause. Whether it was freedom, the spiritual well-being of others, higher education, or even the abolition of slavery, each ancestor had seemed driven to pursue an undeniably noble end.

Coming of age in the modern world, various pressures have a way of eclipsing the noble causes of our times. Our culture grinds hard against those who would pursue anything other than the well trodden path toward financial security and the tranquility offered by an upper-middle-class suburban lifestyle. In addition to such cultural pressures it seems that for every would-be noble cause there are a host of voices arguing against any end it might seek to accomplish.

Even at a young age it became obvious to me that the absolutes which inspired the pursuits of my ancestors were no longer agreed upon.

For some time I wrestled with the issues of meaning and purpose. For every large question I asked, modern society seemed to offer a neatly-packaged answer that had been well accepted by the people I most admired. In time I became convinced that with the exception of a few pressing international and domestic problems, which seemed at the brink of being solved, few significant challenges aside from continued technological advancement remained. As I grew older, adult complacency slowly replaced youthful idealism and I began to conform to the pattern of the modern world. It really did seem as though all the world's dragons had been slain and that it was now the lot of men to woo women and enjoy the spoils of war won by those who had fought in ages long past.

I must admit that throughout those years I possessed a restless spirit. It was as if something deep inside me was forcing me to remember and to attempt to fulfill my childhood dreams of making a difference in the world, of investing my life in something with immense significance. I reasoned that hard work and the determination to pursue enough wealth to ensure a comfortable lifestyle would eventually satisfy any such deep-seated longing. Several years of pursuing the "American Dream," however, did little to satisfy that visceral hunger to discover and pursue my noble cause.

Made for This

Up to this point in my life journey I had been traveling solo. My hopes and dreams had been mine to pursue alone. In 1982, however, I had the privilege of marrying a woman who shared my outlook on life. Together we faced the challenges common to young couples and continued together in our pursuit of "the good life." Just how good life can really be was revealed to us a few short months after our marriage. Lonely for significant friendships we decided on a whim to attend a local church one Sunday morning. After the service a young associate pastor asked if we would like to join the church softball team. Avid athletes, we enthusiastically jumped at the offer.

A few weeks into the softball season our pastor friend invited us to his home to enjoy dinner with him and his wife. A pleasant evening eventually came to a close and as we prepared to travel home the pastor handed me a small booklet, requesting that I read it and that we could, perhaps, discuss its contents at some point. And so it was that I held in my hands for the first time the Gospel of John.

From the moment I began reading the pages of that booklet I have never been the same. My heart melted away as I came face-to-face with the answers for which I had been searching all my life. It was as if God had written this letter just for me. I began to see reality with a degree of clarity I had never thought possible. Over the next few months my wife and I surrendered our hearts to the Lord in faith and began a journey of discipleship that continues to this day.

As a new believer I could not get enough of God's Word. At every opportunity I continued my way systematically through all that God had to share with those who would listen. It was clear very early on that I had found my passion, and it was with a sense of deep joy that I discovered that my wife shared it with me. To know Christ and to please Him was the new focus of our life together.

After coming to faith in Christ my burning desire was to discover just how it was that my wife and I could serve Him in the world today. I would begin each morning by asking Jesus to make our life direction clear. I had no desire to proceed in dim shadows at this point, and so promised that if He led clearly I would follow faithfully. My friends now jokingly remind me that maturity in the Lord has a way of making one cautious concerning praying for life direction. As a new believer some twenty years ago, however, I had not yet learned this, and so my boldness in prayer continued daily for some months.

Before long an unmistakable direction became apparent. At first it came through Paul's writings. Later I sensed it thematically across the whole of Scripture. God's heart for the world was very clear. His desire that every nation be presented with the truth of biblical faith seemed to leap off each page. It all made perfect sense as I read Paul's words in the tenth chapter of Romans concerning the reality that people cannot come to faith if no one is sent to share the truth with them.

Sharing these thoughts with mature Christians whom I had come to respect brought confirmation. Many who knew me well clearly recognized how God had been preparing me all my life for this direction – this calling to bring the gospel to people in lands where it had yet to be carried. Considering these facts it dawned on me that I had finally found what I had been searching for since childhood. I had become passionate in my pursuit of the Lord, and had discovered, at long last, my noble quest. With a sense of deep satisfaction I realized that the Lord had created me for this very purpose.

Searching for Direction

I suppose it is true of many boys who were raised listening with eager ears to accounts of heroic soldiers that we see any worthwhile struggle as a battle. This outlook remains a deep part of my personality, and so when searching for a place to bring the gospel I wanted the most difficult battle situation available. Where, I wondered, had the message of biblical faith made the fewest inroads? Were there still peoples in far-off lands who have yet to hear? Were there still wars to be fought for the souls of men?

With such questions burning in my mind I scheduled an interview with a man who was well known in our community as a biblical scholar and historian. I did not know him well personally, yet felt sure that with all his knowledge he could point me in the right direction if nothing else. Looking back I realize that he was known for his academic studies rather than his travels or familiarity with world events, and that this fact may account for the direction he offered.

I shared with this gentleman how I had sensed a calling from the Lord to bring the gospel to peoples in a foreign land who had not yet had the opportunity to hear it, and that I had been encouraged to pursue this direction by mature Christians with whom I had been studying and worshiping for many months. With great anticipation I finally asked: "Are there still places in the world today where the gospel has not yet been shared?" I remember as if it were yesterday how this wise man pondered my question for some time. At long last he began to speak as I listened with rapt attention. "No, I don't think so. As far as I know there is a church in every country on earth, and so there is little left for us to do in these regards."

I suppose it was the authority with which he uttered the statement that unnerved me most. Had I been born too late? Was the direction I sensed from the Lord misguided? Could it really be that there were no battles left for me to join? Crushed, I returned home to consider what I had been told.

My situation at this point resembled a man who after traveling for some time now found himself facing a fork in the road. My spiritual mentors assured me that I had been misguided, that there remained many places around the world where the gospel had not yet been received, and yet it was they who suggested I seek counsel from this learned man. I had no intention of going forward without clear direction. The last thing I wanted was to invest my life in a half-hearted effort to do something that sounded spiritual, yet was of little eternal value.

One Sunday morning after attending a service I stood contemplating such issues as others enjoyed coffee and donuts in the fellowship hall. Stepping outside for a breath of fresh air I was confronted by a very strange looking man. Tall and dark, his long black hair and heavy beard had obviously not been given much attention in weeks. With his thin body dressed in torn brown clothes he stood there, with an orange in his hand, staring at me. He was the picture of intensity. His eyes seemed to see right through me, and it was as if he knew what I had been thinking moments before.

Certain I had stumbled into the path of a homeless wanderer, I uttered some polite greeting and wondered what sort of response I would receive. Ignoring my words he began quoting passages of Scripture. I could barely keep up with him, yet as he spoke he identified the passages as coming from the writings of Isaiah. He went on and on about islands and nations, and the Lord's message and judgment and battles. Every few moments he would stop and ask how I planned to respond to God's call.

It was unmistakably clear that this intense stranger was challenging me to fulfill the Lord's plan to reach the nations. Having been brought up in New England, however, I had never been confronted in such a bold manner. I had no clue how to respond, and so with all the courage I could muster I asked if he would like another orange. Not waiting for a response I turned and walked a few yards to the table upon which various bowls of fruit had been placed. As I turned back, fruit in hand, the man was gone. I entered the fellowship hall, and then walked around the buildings, but no matter where I looked the man was not to be found, nor had anyone else seemed to have seen him.

I honestly had no idea what to make of this strange encounter, yet it did serve to make me think. As I considered the man's words, it was clear he was saying that the battle is by no means over, and that the war for the souls of men rages on to this day. With renewed optimism, I continued daily to ask the Lord for direction.

Not long after this discussion I was given a book that mentioned an organization known as The US Center for World Mission, located in Pasadena, California. I wrote to them and received a catalog of publications. Almost every title seemed aimed at answering the questions I had been asking with regard to the remaining task of world missions.

These publications made it clear that when God looks at the world He sees it very different from the way we have arranged things. Whereas we have divided the world into some two hundred or so political units recognized by the United Nations, God sees mankind as belonging to ethnic groups. The word used in Scripture which is generally translated "nations" is actually the Greek term "ethnos" from which we derive the word ethnic. In other words, whereas one might look at the world in terms of recognized political units and argue that each nation has been "reached" with the gospel to at least some degree, when the world is divided into ethnic groups, or cultures separated from one another by linguistic or other criteria, it is clear that much remains to be accomplished.

The term "people group" is used to refer to what has become a new way for us to look at nations of the world. As one begins to study populations on the basis of language alone, there are today some seven thousand unique languages spoken. Each language represents people who consider themselves distinct from other peoples based on their common language and culture. A "nation" such as Thailand, for example, while considered one country on maps, may actually be home to several people groups, each with its own language and culture. I was surprised to learn that many people groups have populations numbering in the millions.

As researchers began breaking down the world in this way it quickly became apparent that hundreds of these people groups have little or no Christian witness. There are dozens of groups to this day, some comprised of millions of individuals, who have no indigenous church capable of reaching their own people with the message of biblical faith. Known as "unreached people groups," without outside efforts the people within these populations will most likely never have an opportunity to hear and respond to the gospel.

After learning these facts my direction became abundantly clear. There was no doubt in my mind that the Lord had made me for the purpose of investing my life so that a people could be offered the Truth. I began pouring over volumes containing lists and descriptions of unreached people groups. My goal was to find the group which represented the most people who had the least chance to hear. In short, I wanted more than anything else to discover the toughest battle I could find – to join those who were struggling against the longest odds. My thinking was that I could be of most use by going where few others dared venture.

Finding an unreached people group to work among is not a difficult task. It is estimated that only five percent of all missions efforts are targeted at unreached people groups. The vast majority of missionaries have significant and valuable ministries working within groups that have been reached for many years, yet for one reason or another still require outside assistance.

The five percent focusing on unreached peoples concentrate their efforts on only a very small percentage of Islamic peoples. The reasons are not difficult to understand. These people are not only unreached, they aggressively want to stay this way.

Research into Islam and Islamic peoples proved fascinating. The first surprising aspect involved population statistics. Today there are well over a billion Muslims living throughout the world. It has been estimated that one out of every three to four people in the world now claims adherence to the religion of Islam. Moreover, statistics indicate that through a combination of birth rate and evangelism Islam is growing at a rate equal to or greater than any other major religion in the world. Not only are Islamic peoples unreached, therefore, but they are doing an outstanding job of reaching the world for Islam.

Another interesting aspect with regard to Islam is the manner in which Islamic populations are shielded from outside influences. Whereas blocks of other unreached people groups may be separated from the gospel through linguistic or other cultural barriers, many Islamic populations have purposefully and even proactively shielded their members from exposure to the message of biblical faith.

Understanding, then, that Islamic peoples account for up to one-third of the world's population, and that many such peoples have little or no chance for exposure to the gospel, I strongly sensed I was headed in the right direction. My strong desire to discover where it is I was most needed, to find a battle that represented significant eternal consequences, had been met in Islam. I very much sensed that investing my life so that an Islamic people group could be offered the message of biblical faith is what the Lord would have me pursue. Remembering my commitment to follow faithfully as the Lord led clearly, I could hardly wait to begin.

Chapter Two

Forward in Faith

S haring the direction I sensed with my wife as the months unfolded, she agreed, somewhat reluctantly, that the Lord had very clearly answered our prayers for direction. The confirmations were so unmistakably clear and the direction so evident, that she too could not help but see that this was of the Lord.

To this day my wife is often asked if, looking back, she sensed a "call" as strongly as I did. She always answers that her clear call was and is to be the wife God called her to be. She never sensed that God wanted her as an individual to "reach" Islamic groups, but that He wanted her to be a faithful wife. This she has been and I give her a tremendous amount of credit for standing strong through many situations that have caused strong men to fold. I cannot recall one time during the past sixteen years when she has complained about our living conditions or the security of our family.

Having grown in the Lord for three years and sensing such clear leading, I began in the mid-1980s writing to every missions agency whose address I could find. Each one required that we have at least a year of Bible and missions training before any further steps toward the missions field could be taken.

With this in mind we put our home on the market, resigned from our positions at local banking institutions, and headed off to Columbia, South Carolina, to attend a one-year Bible and Missions Certificate program. Our time at Bible college was thrilling. The professors were godly men and women, many of whom had served overseas for years. The wise counsel and excellent instruction we received allowed us to grow and expand our vision significantly.

An added benefit of attending such an institution is the fact that missions agencies regularly visit in an effort to recruit students for overseas assignments. Almost every week we would, along with several other couples and singles, be treated to dinner by a missions representative. I would ask the same question of each one: "What is involved in the process of opening a new work among an unreached people group." At that time the "people group" paradigm was rather new to the missions community. This was especially true for the more established agencies which had been sending people out for many decades.

The answer to my question generally involved years of working on an established field which had been "reached" many years before. This was followed by a few years of red tape before a new endeavor could be considered by those in authority over regions in which the new work would take place. We would always politely thank our host for the meal, and then return home shaking our heads in amazement that such important work would take so long to get started. I began to wonder if all missions endeavors operated with such breakneck lethargy and bureaucratic protocol.

One day as our time at Bible college was coming to a close, I noticed an announcement for a meal hosted by the director of a relatively new missions agency. The set-up was strange for two reasons. First, I had never heard of a director hosting such a meeting, and second, I think the meal offered was sandwiches rather than a full dinner. Whether for these reasons or because the agency was quite unknown at the time, I believe my wife and I were the only "potential recruits" who showed up. We had a wonderful time getting to know the director and his wife. They seemed so much more ordinary than many we had met over the months. This may be due to the fact that the gentleman had been an executive in the business world for many years.

For whatever reason, we felt more comfortable during this meeting than we had at any other such event. After a time of becoming acquainted, I finally asked the question I had asked so many times in the past regarding how we could begin a work among an unreached people group. As it turns out this agency had been founded on the people group paradigm, and everything was geared toward sending teams out to begin new efforts. The director's answer was fast and clear: "You gather a qualified team backed by strong churches to target an unreached people, develop a workable strategy no matter how unconventional, and you go!"

It was as if at long last we finally found someone else who

spoke our language. As we continued talking, everything having to do with this agency made so much sense. The bureaucratic overkill common to missions had been replaced by a more business-like model. The hallmarks were flexibility, creativity, and dependence upon God. We signed on that very evening and have been with this agency for more than sixteen years now.

Over the next few weeks we learned that three couples had recently formed a team targeting one of the most populous and unreached Islamic people groups in the world. We agreed to join the team for a year in order to "feel out" whether or not it targeted the group we sensed the Lord would have us serve.

Initial Encounters

As one who had never left the east coast of the United States I was not prepared for what confronted us as we landed in the capital city of a bustling Islamic nation. Having set things up in such a way that we would make our way alone to the distant city in which our team members had recently taken up residence, we had no clue which way to turn.

There was absolutely nothing familiar about the scenes that confronted us. To make things a bit more interesting, it turns out that our flight landed at 11:00pm local time. Wandering the streets of this dark city, stopped here and there by locals who spoke no English, we were terrified.

We eventually found lodging for the evening, and after a few days made our way to the home of our team leader. Over the next few weeks we settled into the home of a local Muslim family and began the process of language learning and cultural adjustment.

As the months unfolded there was no question that we were exactly where the Lord wanted us. Our initial terror was slowly replaced by an ever-expanding familiarity with, and appreciation for, the culture, and our acquisition of the language proceeded slowly but surely. We eventually did a good bit of traveling to other areas in order to familiarize ourselves with other unreached Islamic people groups of the region. As we approached the end of our initial year we strongly sensed we had found the region where the Lord would have us invest our lives.

The next step was to discover how we could best contribute to the efforts aimed at reaching the people of this region with the gospel, and how to obtain permission from the department of immigration to stay in country on a long-term basis. As it turns out the answer to both questions involved the same path.

Over the year we became very close friends with both our team members and a few missionary couples who had served in the region for many years. As we discussed our next move with these people, one who had lived in the region for decades made a somewhat surprising suggestion. Taking account of my gifting and interests, he challenged me to return to the United States to begin work on a degree in cultural anthropology.

He patiently explained that one reason so little had been accomplished in the region for the Kingdom of God despite many years of efforts is that very few of those working in the area had taken the opportunity to study the culture by working with its leaders. For years the approach had been to work with peasants and others at the lower end of the social hierarchy because they had proven to be the ones most open to change. He suggested that returning to work in the country as an anthropologist with proper credentials would open doors to leaders never before available to missionaries and would result in valuable insights regarding how the gospel can best take root within the cultures of the region.

The suggestion made perfect sense from a strategic standpoint and also answered the question of how a long-term visa could be obtained. The fact is that one cannot simply show up in an Islamic nation and announce that he or she is a missionary and would like permission to stay. The nicest thing that would happen in such circumstances would be an escort to the international airport. With this in mind any foreigner wishing to reside in such countries must be creative in an effort to justify his or her long-term residence. Tourist and social visit visas only last so long, and so various other options such as business or educational opportunities must be pursued. A research visa for an anthropologist made perfect sense for long-term residence requirements.

The strategic and long-term residency value of the plan made a great deal of sense to all involved in the discussion, as did the fit with my personality, interests, and the manner in which I enjoyed long discussions with Muslims. As we prayed for confirmation for this new direction, the Lord made our path very clear just as he had done for each step thus far. My disappointment in having to delay beginning a work among a new people group of the region was offset by the practical value the plan held for opening doors to work with men at the very highest levels of the social hierarchy.

Returning to the States, I entered a university that accepted most of my work at Bible college for credit. Working diligently for two years or so, I returned to the Islamic nation to conduct fieldwork for one year toward my undergraduate honors thesis.

During this year my wife and I lived with a very important Muslim leader and his family in one of the region's urban areas. We grew very close to this family in many ways and had ample opportunity to discuss spiritual issues. It was during this time that my wife became pregnant with our first child, and this situation seemed to endear us all the more to the man and his family. It did not take long for our hosts to begin taking on the role of future grandparents. The manner in which women in the culture handle pregnancy is very different from the western routines. This fact made for some interesting and amusing times over the ensuing months.

Highly educated and well placed within the community, the father of the family was very candid with regard to how I should proceed in my studies. "If you really want to understand the people of this region," he suggested, "you have to gain access to the fundamentalist Islamic leaders. A handful of these men represent millions of followers who would die at a moments notice for them. They are the ones who hold the keys to this culture."

Over the next few months I began focusing on these groups and the men who lead them. Sure enough, everywhere I looked I began to see signs indicating that what I had been told was exactly correct. Once I knew what to look for I could tell which areas were under the leadership of which leaders. I made several attempts to learn more about these large Islamic organizations, yet I could only go so far as an "outsider."

As I gained as much information as I could concerning these fundamentalist Islamic groups and the men who led them, my future direction became very clear. Somehow I would have to gain access to these leaders. As my year of fieldwork came to an end, I realized these men represented my new target group, and I began praying for a way to return and work among them.

Road Blocks

Upon returning to the United Sates my wife gave birth to our first child. As I finished my undergraduate work, our second child made our family of four complete. As new parents we looked forward to all the Lord had in store for us as we continued to follow His direction for our lives.

After receiving my undergraduate degree, I began searching for an outstanding graduate program in cultural anthropology. My goal was to enter a well-respected program in one of the nation's top secular universities. Being affiliated with such an institution, I reasoned, would help my chances of gaining access to the men I had chosen to work among.

My grades were excellent and the fact that I had significant fieldwork experience was quite unusual. That my transcripts showed a year of studies undertaken at a Bible college, however, worked against me. One must understand that the discipline of anthropology is, to a large extent, closely tied with evolutionary and other theories that for most anthropologists stand in stark contrast to biblical teachings. This being the case my chances of being accepted into the anthropology department of a major university were significantly less than would be the case for one whose transcripts did not show evidence of time at a Bible college. After sending in five or so applications, however, I followed them up with phone calls to the department heads who had the final decision concerning who would enter their particular program. The university that represented my top choice had six or so openings for new graduate students and several hundred applicants. Every few weeks I would call and ask how many openings still remained and whether or not I had been chosen for one of them. By the time only one opening remained, I offered to fly out for a personal interview with the director. I suspect he agreed simply in an effort to stop my phone calls.

The interview went well. At one point, however, the professor asked me to "explain this Bible college thing." I made clear that I do, in fact, live my life based on the teachings of the Bible, yet that my beliefs had not stopped me from thriving within a secular anthropology department during my undergraduate career. The recommendations from my former professors bore this fact out. They characterized me as a serious student with unique perspectives. To this day I suspect I was given that last opening as something of a dare to find out how long I could last with the "big boys" of anthropology.

The first few semesters at graduate school went very well. I held my own in debates and was quickly accepted as a serious member of the academic community. My beliefs did not seem to be a stumbling block to anyone, and the opportunities for meeting important visiting and resident leaders from the Islamic nation on which I had been focusing were plentiful. I remember thinking how wonderfully the entire strategy had worked out to that point.

As is true with many major universities, there was a significant international student population on campus. I quickly became closely associated with the student group representing what by that time had become "my second nation." Speaking their language and having lived in their homeland, they treated me very well. My wife and I established significant friendships during those days that continue today.

Everything seemed to be working out very smoothly. As time wore on I looked forward to returning overseas and working with the men I had targeted some time earlier. My graduate career was progressing at a fast pace, and it looked as if I would finish the program a year or so ahead of my colleagues, most of whom had entered without a clear direction in mind.

The first hint of any trouble came one day when I noticed a good friend approaching fast with a very concerned look on his face. He was a professor from the nation I had been focusing on for so long. We had become very close, and I wondered what could be troubling him so deeply. He pushed me off into an empty room and began explaining about a meeting he had just attended. It turned out that a few days earlier an important member of the department's leadership had casually asked him all about our relationship and how my friend would characterize my relationships with the student group from his Islamic nation.

My friend assured the questioning faculty member that I had been well accepted within the group, had helped several of the students in various ways, and had even taken the time to lead a Bible study for several of them from time to time. Thinking he had done me a favor, my friend was sure that I must have been up for some sort of recognition and hoped his words would prove helpful. To his great surprise, he learned a few moments before our chance meeting that his words had been used for quite a different purpose. It turns out that I had been recommended by several committee members for a large financial grant for my upcoming field-work. These funds were sought after by dozens of students.

The committee member who had questioned my friend used his "testimony" to make the case that I was actually a missionary, and that I should, therefore, not be selected to receive the funds. Having been asked by the committee if what he had shared several days earlier was true, that I had been leading Bible studies among students from his Islamic nation, my friend had no choice but to confirm the truth of what he had shared. He explained that in trying to help me, he had quite possibly just ruined my graduate career.

Not long thereafter I was called in for a meeting with the program director. He explained that he knew I was a Christian when he accepted me into the department, yet had not suspected that I was a missionary. He went on to say what I already knew too well, that missionaries are loathed by anthropologists as those who spoil other cultures by introducing foreign beliefs and practices. He made it very clear in a rather indirect way that it would be difficult from this point on for me to receive the assistance enjoyed by most doctoral candidates with regard to funding and the institutional sponsorship necessary to work in other nations.

It had been almost six years since the suggestion was first made that I return to the United States and focus on earning a degree in cultural anthropology that would allow me to work with men at the highest levels of leadership within the Islamic people groups we had targeted. Everything to this point had worked very smoothly. I had spent time with leaders who had visited the university and had established close relationships with graduate students who would soon return to this nation to fill important positions in government and various universities. I felt certain that with such connections I would be able to work my way into a position of being able to get at least close to some of the less important leaders of the fundamentalist groups, and that over time my reputation and contacts might allow me to eventually meet some of the top men. Now, however, everything seemed to have come crashing down in the space of a week, and I wondered if I would ever even be allowed to return to the land of my calling. It looked very much like six years of patient work and financial sacrifice had been wasted.

Not knowing how to proceed, I called the pastor of our home church several states away. A mature man of God and good friend, our pastor was thoroughly familiar with, and very supportive of, the path we had taken over the years. His advice was to patiently proceed with our plans and watch for how the Lord would open doors. His thought was that since the Lord had led us so clearly to this point, it was obviously His will that we continue. I must admit this advice sounded very simplistic given the severity of the issues involved. I wondered if he had no idea what to say and so just said whatever sounded spiritually uplifting for the moment. Thinking back on the close walk this man enjoys with our Lord, however, I sensed I should follow his advice no matter how simplistic it sounded.

These circumstances represented a turning point in my walk with the Lord. After much struggle in prayer and many hours spent searching for answers in the Bible, I came to the realization that I had been motivated all these years by my longing to see Muslims come to Christ. In short I was doing all this for my love of the people whom I had targeted. The Lord used the realization on my part that I might never be able to return to them to show me that this motivation represented a subtle shift from my original motives – my desire to please the Lord through honoring His Word. I realized that though subtle, this shift was a dangerous one.

I soon came to the point of not caring so much about my grand plan to save the world. I slowly came back to placing the Lord in His proper place as my first love. After doing so my spiritual life became characterized by a freedom I had not known in years. I realized afresh that circumstances mean very little in light of being vitally united in a relationship with Christ. With renewed passion for Christ I took my pastor's advice and kept working, not having any idea what the Lord had in store for the months to come.

Open Doors

The irony of this situation involves the manner in which the Lord would not allow me to fulfill my strong desire to return overseas until the very moment I was willing to trade that desire for a renewed passion for Him. It seemed He was making it very clear that He would not allow me to return until my relationship with Him had been restored to what it had once been. Looking back I can see the necessity of this subtle yet profound adjustment. Had I gone forth motivated by my love for Muslims, what would have happened, I wonder, during the many short yet very real times over the years when my love for the people seemed to vanish altogether? To this day I often speak with missionary colleagues who clearly operate motivated by love for the people they serve. When it seems appropriate, I gently share my story of how the Lord dealt with me severely to help me realize the subtle difference between a passion for the people and a right relationship with Him.

The time for my fieldwork was fast approaching and I knew I could not count on the university for the sponsorship necessary to work overseas or for assistance in obtaining a long-term research visa. I had no idea how these very real problems would be solved yet continued looking for the open doors my pastor had promised. Major decisions would have to be made very soon with regard to the next steps, and yet I knew very well that without some breakthrough I would not be able to return to the work I strongly sensed the Lord had prepared for me to do.

With about two months remaining, I could see no prospect of open doors. I had continued my relationships with the international students I had come to know and love, and during a meeting one of them approached me. He was a very bright Muslim working on a graduate degree in history.

He mentioned that he met a man from his country at a seminar on Islamic studies in another city, and that he had shared some of my writings with him. The paper he shared concerned the Islamic organizations I hoped to study during my fieldwork.

I later learned that the man to whom the papers were given did a good deal of background work on me. He interviewed many of my friends to determine what I was like and whether or not I could be trusted. Apparently satisfied, he eventually sought me out.

We were introduced by our mutual friend. I was immediately impressed with this man I judged to be a quiet intellectual. I shall refer to him here as Ahmed. As is common in most conversations with people of this region, the initial small talk lasted for hours before anything of substance could be discussed. I eventually learned that Ahmed worked as a professor of languages in a university located in the very area in which I hoped to work. Moreover, I discovered that he belonged in some capacity to the largest fundamentalist Islamic organization in the region. In fact, his relationship with the organization in question concerned the reason he had desired to meet me.

It turns out that the various Islamic organizations scattered across the region have very interesting relationships with one another. On one level there is a great deal of cooperation and brotherhood, and yet on another there is a concern with regard to establishing and maintaining a reputation for significance. Ahmed belonged to one of the largest groups in the region. It had a reputation for extreme fundamentalism. One might even go so far as to say that the millions involved were viewed by outsiders as fanatics. And yet there was a growing concern on the part of some of the leaders that other groups had no idea just how orthodox, or theologically sound for lack of a better term understandable to the western mind, the organization had become over the years.

It was something of an embarrassment for members of this group to travel to other areas only to hear their group being spoken of as less than orthodox by fellow Muslims. Ahmed himself had experienced this. When he read my paper, he wondered if I would be interested in working among the leadership of this and other similar groups so that I could then write about all that had been accomplished over the years, and just how truly orthodox they had become. Ahmed explained that as a member of the faculty at the most prestigious university in the area, he would be delighted to offer me sponsorship to undertake this fieldwork in his home nation.

I have mentioned throughout this work that since coming to faith in Christ I have felt very clearly led concerning what He would have me do to serve Him. My prayer has always been for clear direction, and He has honored my desires in this regard. Yet never had I more clearly seen an open door placed in my path as I did during the conversation noted above. A major obstacle to my returning overseas had just been blown away. Moreover, the open door offered to me by this Muslim gentleman led directly to the leaders I had targeted several years before. My thoughts often return to my pastor's advice when I think of this moment, and I have pledged to listen very carefully the next time he offers his view.

Ahmed was also at the point of finishing his graduate

studies and would be returning home soon. I mentioned that his proposal held certain points of interest, and that I hoped it would work out for us to work together in the future – no sense appearing too enthusiastic in such circumstances!

There was still the issue of a research visa. Sponsorship from Ahmed's university solved a major problem, yet the normal process for foreign researchers involved obtaining a visa on the recommendation of the director of the researcher's graduate program. Sensing it was pointless to seek this and that it might even lead to further complications, I wondered how this remaining obstacle would be overcome.

Most of the students belonging to the international group representing our adopted nation were single. We spent a good deal of time together at various events, but I suppose I was in many ways closest to a man who, like me, was married and had two children. Our families would often get together for outings, and we all grew to be close friends. My wife particularly enjoyed practicing her language skills with his wife. I believe it was at the birthday party of this man's daughter that we sat chatting during the last few weeks of my final semester.

I knew Saleh was a devout Muslim, and that he had been studying for his doctorate in history. He had held many jobs over the years, but I was not very clear on what his latest job back in his home country had been. He asked what I planned to do about my fieldwork. I shared how one of his countrymen had offered me a great opportunity, but that I still needed help getting a research visa. I explained how the few inquiries I had made to date had not even been answered by his government.

He looked at me with the clever smile for which he is well known and said, "Do you have any idea what I do back home?"

"Probably goof off like you do here," I think I said.

"Well, that may be true, but the fact is I still work for the National Science Foundation in my country, and it is this organization that sent me here to finish my doctorate," he explained. "And what is more, just guess what my official position is in that institution?"

Not sure where he was going with all this, I just played along and said nothing.

"I am a member of the committee in charge of granting visas to foreign researchers, and my job is to review their work each quarter to make sure they are doing what it is they say they are doing. Do you understand me? If you go to my country, I'll kind of be your boss. How about that?"

Somewhat skeptical, I explained to Saleh that he might never get the chance to lord it over me since I had no idea how I would get a visa at this point. He asked that I give him a copy of my passport along with a research proposal and the letter which Ahmed had sent me offering official sponsorship. He then boasted that he would take care of the rest at record speed. Within a day or so I had the paperwork for him, yet knowing Saleh as a man who enjoys a reputation as a great exaggerator, I had my doubts that he could actually deliver on his promise. In fact, I was not even sure whether or not to believe what he said about his position. It just seemed a bit too coincidental that he would actually be the one man in the world who could help me at this particular moment in time and space.

Over the next few days Saleh spent more than a dozen hours making international telephone calls, sending faxes, and hosting conference calls. True to his word he got my research visa approved in just a few weeks, whereas even those who go through the official university channels generally wait up to six months. Moreover, he noted that the director of the National Science Foundation in his country was looking forward to meeting me soon, and that based on Saleh's excellent recommendation, this man would personally help me in any way possible.

I marveled at how God had arranged things in order to overcome what I considered to be yet another insurmountable obstacle. Remembering how just a few months earlier I had no hope of returning overseas, I now had a personal invitation to work with the most prominent Islamic leaders in the region, with the blessings of the director of the nation's National Science Foundation. More importantly, I had been freed from my burden of having to reach these people for Christ. I was now free to enjoy watching Christ work through me as I sought to abide in Him.

Chapter Three

A Whole New World

It had been more than a dozen years since my wife and I first came to faith in Christ. To date we had spent two years in the Islamic nation that would become our adopted home and many years planning our return. We realized, however, that the open doors through which we were about to pass were nothing like those we had entered before.

For one thing, we now had two very young children. Life as a couple has certain advantages when living in challenging situations over attempting the same feats as a family of four. In addition, we very clearly realized that the people whom we would work among were not the same as those we had come to know so well.

Subtle Distinctions

With a population of some 1.4 billion people scattered

across much of the earth, the world of Islam can be difficult to comprehend. When most scholars are asked to divide the world of Islam into categories they usually do so along the lines of what have become the major "theological" branches of the faith. One hears of Sunnis and Shiites and of the mystic Sufis known for their unusual styles of worship. As a Christian anthropologist, however, I study Islam from a somewhat different vantage point.

Whereas practitioners of the social sciences generally see themselves as detached observers with regard to issues of faith, my devotion to God and adherence to what I believe to be His Word have allowed me a rather unusual view of Islam. Rather than looking down upon them from a post-religious pedestal, I look across to them as fellow worshipers of Almighty God. Without question we understand the way to God very differently, and in all honesty realize that our paths are mutually exclusive with regard to who will actually make it to heaven, yet we are very similar in our devotion to God and our adherence to that which we consider to be His Word.

With this in mind when asked to break down the world of Islam into meaningful categories I do so with regard to how it is Muslims relate to that which they consider to be God's revealed will – the al-Quran. Virtually all Muslims believe that the Quran was revealed to Muhammad almost 1400 years ago, yet the impact it has on their lives today varies a great deal. I will go into detail regarding these differences in a later chapter. For now it is sufficient to understand that I consider it most helpful to perceive Muslims as belonging to either cultural, Quranic, or militant Islam. It is important, however, to realize that although these categories are useful for understanding principles common to Muslims within each grouping, they by no means represent clearly-delineated categories to which one might claim adherence.

By a wide margin most Muslims in the world today would fall into the first category. Like their counterparts in what might be referred to as "cultural Christianity," most cultural Muslims were born into their faith. The majority reside in Islamic areas of the world and live according to the customs of their land. They may be very familiar with well-known passages from the Quran and may have even studied it in their youth, yet it does not serve as the central determining factor for life decisions. Those within this category are concerned with the more practical issues of life, tending to adhere to the normative behavioral patterns of their contemporary fellow citizens, which in turn are based on the lives of their ancestors, which certainly, they would suggest, were based on Quranic teachings.

The second category, that which I call Quranic Islam, is roughly equivalent to what one might label biblical Christianity. Those within this grouping take the teachings of the Quran very seriously. Many spend a great deal of time studying the Quran and Hadith, a vast collection of ancient writings concerning the life of Muhammad. Individuals falling within this category consider the teachings of the Quran relevant for today and actively seek to live their lives accordingly.

The remaining category, militant Islam, will be dealt with in a later chapter. I mention these categories now to highlight the fact that whereas our previous residency had been among those belonging to cultural and Quranic Islam, we clearly understood that we would now be entering an area in which militant Islam had made significant inroads, and that a good part of my fieldwork would take place within Islamic educational institutions the western press now refers to as terrorist training camps.

Being There

Some of the more imaginative among us enjoy dreaming about what life would be like if time travel were possible. "Just think," they muse, "what it would be like to live in an ancient civilization like Egypt with the pharaohs, and how life would be different for a commoner in lands untouched by modern conveniences. How incredibly fascinating it would be to just sit and watch such civilizations unfold over time!" The fact is that several "exotic civilizations" like those generally considered to be relegated to ancient history still exist in parts of the world today. To be honest, it was with the same sense of fascination noted above that I "watched" the world to which my family and I were transported for my fieldwork.

It is difficult to put into words what one feels as he begins life in such a setting. Having studied Islam from many perspectives from afar had not prepared me for the emotional aspects of how it would be to live among Muslims in a "kingdom-like" setting. I use this term because it best describes the sense of inclusion enjoyed by the members of the community, as well as the intense devotion they have for their spiritual leaders and the common purposes toward which they struggle. As an American growing up in suburbia, and even as a member of evangelical Christianity, I had no frame of reference with which to compare what I was experiencing. I had never been among a group of people so totally committed to their way of life. The term "intoxicating" is the best I can offer to describe this new world in which I found myself.

Just think for a moment what it would be like to be one of millions who share a common struggle and destiny. To "belong" to a religious community whose roots run deep through the centuries and whose branches seek to encompass the whole of humanity. Imagine feeling solid concrete walls reverberate as one is surrounded by many thousands of Muslims chanting Arabic verse in unison while swept away in intense worship. Regardless of background, a visitor experiencing such a scene is easily overcome with a deep sense of awe. Words cannot convey the visceral power which is present at such a time and place.

When worship gives way to discussion and issues of the day are debated, there are, of course, disagreements and divisions over various lesser questions of faith and life. Yet these in no way diminish devotion to the community of faith. Rugged individualism is unknown here. Consensus rules in this setting where devotion to, and sacrifice for, the group represents the norm.

Among such communities individuals who seem to be chosen by God for greatness eventually arise. Sometimes these are men of action. Those who sacrifice their lives for the group are held in high esteem. This is especially the case when one performs heroic deeds against those who have been named enemies of Islam. Individuals who stand up to such threats are remembered in myth and legend long after they depart the earth. Such men, however, are not the most revered. Those who seem to be set apart to lead others to a deeper understanding of Islam are the men who are recalled with the most reverence. A handful of these men have gone on to attract enormous followings and have engendered intense loyalty on the part of those who join their organizations. The desire to discover principles and practices common to such men is what brought me to the world of "fundamentalist" Islam.

My purpose was to discover and document how these spiritual leaders become so very popular, and how they inspire such passionate devotion on the part of those who follow them. In short, I wondered how one who is born in the ordinary manner ends up with millions of followers who are willing to give their very lives for the community of faith to which they belong.

I clearly understood that my official role was that of an anthropologist. Cultural anthropologists study language, religion, and a host of other aspects surrounding the life ways of peoples living in various parts of the world. The core methodology involves what is known as "participant observation." The goal is to go as "deep" as possible within the particular culture in order to better understand the world-view of its members and ultimately add to the understanding of mankind in general. As a well-trained anthropologist, I very much wanted to fulfill this role. And yet as a follower of Christ, I had other motives as well.

The opportunity to study such a society and its leaders

represented a very unusual chance to gain insight into principles common to spiritual movements among Muslims.
With a few relatively small exceptions, biblical faith has not
made inroads into this or any other Islamic region to a significant degree. The opportunity to discover principles
which might one day change this fact represented a thrilling
challenge to me. The added privilege of being able to represent Christ to these men and their followers made this
extraordinary endeavor all the more attractive.

Close Encounters

It is often said that it doesn't matter who you are, but who
you know. What may be considered a simple cliché in some
places proved to be of critical importance in this setting.
One might imagine how much success I would have had
arriving in the community described above as a complete
outsider. It would have taken me many years, if indeed it
were even possible, to establish the trust necessary to gain
the sort of insights for which I had come. As it turns out,
Ahmed spared me this trouble.

Shortly after arriving in the country I stood in the doorway of Ahmed's humble home. I paused for some time
wondering what would happen after making my presence
known. We had only met once, and that was months before
and an entire world away in the United States. Would he
even be home? And if not, what would I do to explain my
presence here to complete strangers?

While standing in the small doorway considering these
questions for some time, events began to unfold which made

any thought of turning back impossible. A pair of huge, dark eyes filled with fear stared at me from a few feet away. A child in the course of running around the home to escape a pursuing cousin had just discovered a strange creature from another planet standing very close to his front door, apparently lost in thought. The situation was made even more uncomfortable for us both since the child's momentum had carried him very close beside me before he could manage to come to a complete stop. Before I could utter a word the frightened youth fled in the opposite direction. Screaming in horror, he raced into a side entrance of the home followed by a gang of small friends who had witnessed the encounter. Cries of what in the local vernacular means "stranger, stranger," the term can also be translated "alien," rang out from the youngsters.

Earlier, I had been glad that I was able to approach the home quietly, relatively unnoticed by those milling around the small confines of the area. Now, however, squinting eyes from every direction focused in on me. Certain that I could not understand their language, adults quickly began debating out loud the question of who this stranger could possibly be as nervous children tugged at their parent's clothing. "A Syrian, I think" one offered, obviously fooled by my dark hair, mustache, and skin tanned by the region's scorching sun. The intense scrutiny made my heart pound. Perspiration collected on my brow as I turned to see the door to the home slowly open. More dark, fearful eyes, this time belonging to a veiled woman. Muffled calls for the man of the house followed as I was invited into a small greeting room.

After what seemed like an eternity Ahmed finally

rounded the corner. The recognition in his eyes was instant and very much welcome on my part. I was then embraced as if I were a long lost brother who had returned home after years of wandering some far-off desert region. The concern melted from the faces of the children and women who had gathered, and my heart rate returned to the slightly-higher-than-average pace which had become normal for me since arriving in the country.

Ahmed was overjoyed with my arrival. It was as if a piece of the other world to which he belonged during the course of his graduate studies was now present in his very own home. By getting to know me, his family would now have the opportunity to understand a bit more of what it was like for him while living so far away. It dawned on me that it is quite a responsibility to be the sole representative of the western world to the people in Ahmed's circle of influence. In any case it just seemed right to Ahmed that I should be there, and from that moment on our friendship grew.

Before long Ahmed introduced me to several of his friends. I slowly began to be accepted into the community based on my "lengthy" relationship with Ahmed, who himself was highly regarded by many. The suspicion that would normally surround the presence of a westerner in the community quickly gave way to acceptance on the part of those I grew to know. It was rapidly replaced by curiosity of all things western.

I was treated as something of an anomaly. Ahmed's friends felt very comfortable asking me about aspects of the West, and especially the United States, which they loathed. It was as if I were one of them who had been mistakenly brought up in the United States and had now been returned to my proper place in the world. "No," I explained, "not every woman in the United States is as promiscuous as those who appear in Hollywood movies." "I really don't think so" was my response to the questions concerning whether or not Jews controlled Hollywood and secretly ran the United States government and economy. And so it went for weeks and months. The breaking down of stereotypes continued as I had the opportunity to become well acquainted with many in what had become my new circle of friends.

It took no great effort on my part to think of how I might steer conversations toward spiritual issues. For the most part that is all they wanted to talk about. It quickly became obvious that as much as I desired for them to come to faith in Christ, they were genuinely concerned that I throw off my incorrect views of Jesus and begin worshiping God as Muhammad had taught. At times I was begged with tears to submit to what they considered the only Truth. Though interfaith issues continued to come up somewhat regularly, we came to a tacit understanding after a while that although our ways to God were not the same, the devotion we held for our exclusive paths was.

As time went on I began spending most of my "research time" with Ahmed and one of his good friends. I shall refer to him here as Abdul. Introduced to me as an Islamic theologian, I was instantly impressed with this man. His love of life is contagious, and he can alternate back and forth without hesitation between frivolity and intense concentration on topics of a more serious nature. To this day I remain fascinated with Abdul's depth of insight and seemingly inexhaustible knowledge of all things Islamic. I can recall many times when I asked Abdul questions which had drawn blank stares from others. He answered them without delay, and I cannot recall an instance in which such an answer did not turn out to be very accurate after I had a chance to verify it through various other sources. This being the case, Abdul became one of my most trusted informants as the months wore on.

Although the three of us spent considerable time together, I also had opportunities to meet with Ahmed and Abdul separately. When such meetings took place in their homes, it became very obvious to me that both were devoted family men. Their love for their children was very evident, as were the many sacrifices made for their growth and education.

As we spoke about these issues it was explained that while children are a great source of joy in many ways for their parents, they also represent the future of Islam. This being the case their education is a high priority, especially concerning religion. A sense of responsibility with regard to stewardship of the religion is communicated to children in various ways throughout their upbringing. While some grow to pursue what might be considered a more "secular" path, there are many, like Abdul, who grow increasingly interested in studying Islam. Many opportunities exist to fulfill such interests.

As months went by I enjoyed spending time whenever I could with Ahmed and Abdul. Whether meeting for a meal or joining together for lengthy sightseeing adventures, our discussions eventually centered on the topic of the Islamic groups of the region and the men who lead them. When we discussed the possibility of my being able to meet, or even interview, several of the more important men in the region, Abdul assured me that it would not be too much trouble since he was related to several of them. In all our time together he had never mentioned this seemingly insignificant fact. Even now he just threw it out with a mischievous grin on his face, wondering what my reaction would be.

Face to Face

As had been the case when Ahmed had approached me in the United States I marveled at how through no clever manipulation on my part, a man who held the keys to the insights which I sought had been placed along my path. Whereas Ahmed had made it possible for me to be welcomed into a world in which I would otherwise have been treated with mistrust, Abdul, with his blood-ties, now offered me access to circles seldom encountered by those from the western world. Indeed, even important locals would not think it within the realm of possibility to meet one-on-one with several of the most respected Islamic leaders of the region.

As our relationships grew the time finally came when a meeting with a prominent Islamic leader had been set. With the help of my friends I carefully prepared my questions for what I was sure would be a very formal and structured setting. Since I had no clue as to how these leaders would react to my being present in their "inner sanctums" I wanted to ensure I had my questions prioritized should it happen that I be asked to leave after only a short time.

The day for which I had been preparing finally arrived. I

would have the rare opportunity to meet and interview one of the most respected leaders of the region along with a small group of his closest advisors. Armed with my prioritized questions and thankful for the companionship of Ahmed and Abdul, I set out for what I felt sure would be a very interesting encounter.

It took some time to make our way to the headquarters of the leader's organization. As we approached the enormous complex Ahmed and Abdul's excitement was easily discernable. I did a somewhat better job of hiding my emotions.

Entering the walled compound which seemed to have no end, I observed several hundred young people dressed in white from head to toe move purposefully around what appeared to be a campus area. They were apparently moving from one teaching session to another. The students seemed surprised to see a foreign visitor. Some wondered aloud who I could possibly be while others averted their eyes so as not to be rude. I later learned that as well as including a center for worship and administrative offices, most of the headquarters of the leaders in the region also included training centers swollen with thousands of students of all ages. The opportunity to train under the authority of such men is very much desired.

After making our way across a well-swept courtyard we were escorted into a large room with a ceramic-tile floor and columns supporting a modestly-decorated ceiling. The room was empty of furniture with the exception of a carpeted platform at one end, and several area-rugs on the other. As we entered, all bowed to the man seated upon the carpet on the center of the platform. At his sides were seated eight or so teachers. Our small group sat opposite the men and a period of silence followed, broken only by the clearing of throats for several minutes. I wondered how many times over the millennia this "East meets West" scenario had been played out, and how many times such encounters ended well for the lone representative of a far-off land.

The assembled men on the platform did not look particularly overjoyed to be there. Expressionless, they looked us over for some time. I wondered what I had gotten myself into and just how I would get back out if things did not go so well. The silence probably lasted only a few moments, yet it seemed far longer.

Breaking the awkward moment one of the men on the platform solemnly announced that this meeting had been arranged at the request of one who had traveled a long way to have an audience with the leader. Ahmed was then given a chance to speak. He made an extended, ceremonial speech thanking the leader for his graciousness in allowing us the time to meet with him. He then began to explain the identity of the stranger, and why he had traveled such a long distance. It occurred to me that my life was in Ahmed's hands at this moment. I listened carefully as I was introduced as a learned man from America who had spent years mastering the language of the region and researching the history of many Islamic societies. It was noted that few in the United States were acquainted with the glory of Islam, and that perhaps I could be the one to make them aware. Ahmed went on, to my surprise, to share how he had sought me out and invited me to learn first-hand about the community. In short, it came off sounding like I had done them all a great favor in coming so far to learn more about them. Abdul then spoke up to explain what a devoted friend I had become, and that I could be trusted.

The leader, still expressionless, asked Ahmed in a reserved voice whether or not I was a Muslim. Ahmed calmly made clear that I was a devoted adherent to the Christian Book, a very moral man who loved his family, that I had carefully studied the Quran and was very interested in learning more about Islam. Names were then dropped concerning the many people whom I had met over the months, and that I had been accepted as a trusted seeker of truth. A short period of feeling-out followed in which the leader, through those at his sides, answered many of the questions which I had prepared in advance. The nature of my questions seemed to put many on the platform at ease. Before long, closing statements were made, and our highly-structured meeting had come to an end. We were escorted out of the room as I thought over how much of that for which I had come I was able to learn.

As I prepared to leave, Abdul pulled me to one side and enthusiastically explained that we had been invited to a meal with the leader. I had no idea what would follow. I was simply glad at that point that all had gone well so far, and that I had not been killed for saying something wrong during the interview. To my delight I found that quite the opposite had happened. It seems that Ahmed and Abdul had uttered just the right words to cut through the considerable suspicion on the part of those who had gone into the meeting with observable reluctance.

Before I knew what was happening I was escorted into the

home of the leader. A simple dwelling within the compound, the walls of the home were decorated with modest works of art which had been created by shaping letters of the Arabic alphabet into meaningful designs. To my considerable surprise I was led to a spot directly next to the leader, who sat cross-legged on the carpeted floor. The "platform men" from our meeting of a few minutes before, along with Ahmed and Abdul, sat next to us as a circle was created.

Gone were the more ceremonial outer-garments and expressionless faces. In their stead was a relaxed atmosphere in which small talk and jokes were traded. All that was missing was a sofa, television, and a few pizzas to make the scene reminiscent of a Sunday afternoon football party at Bob's house back in Anytown, USA. What had happened, I wondered, between the meeting room and the leader's home in the few moments it took to get there? In any case the change was welcome, and I began to breathe a bit deeper than had been possible for most of the morning.

I took my place and the leader immediately took my arm and held it for some time as he expressed how glad he was that I had come to visit him. Food was set out by a group of women and to my embarrassment the leader took it upon himself to prepare my plate. Each time I finished the contents of the plate during the course of our conversation the man would fill it again and call for more of what I seemed to be enjoying most. After the meal, still seated in our circle, I was introduced to one of the leader's favorite sons – he had several. The leader warmly suggested that the two of us become good friends, and that we learn from one another. The fact that the leader hoped I would eventually become a

Muslim was very evident at this point.

Conversations continued around the room as I thought about how in the space of a few hours I had gone from what seemed like being on trial before a council of elders to something akin to being made an honorary member of a royal family. I am not sure of the exact potion which made the transformation possible, yet from that moment on I was known in the region as a friend of the leader and was treated with respect in an area where name-dropping represents a highly-developed art form.

The scene outlined above was repeated several times with slightly less formality over the next years. In fact, I am quite sure that some of the less significant details mentioned were inadvertently mixed up with those which took place at meetings with other leaders. In any case having the blessings of these men amounted to having the keys to the kingdom as I continued my research among the people of the region, especially the followers of the leaders whom I had come to know.

Reflecting on the lives of these men who are revered by millions, several things they have in common with one another come to mind. Initially, I was most surprised by the reality that success in these circles is measured not by the accumulation of wealth, but by the number of those associated with the leaders and the degree to which such followers are devoted to Islam.

It is almost unthinkable to imagine that a leader within the United States who holds great power over millions of people would not be surrounded by the trappings of monetary wealth. At a minimum, an expensive home and fine car would be called for in such circumstances. And yet as I spent more time among these Islamic leaders the humble circumstances in which they live never ceased to amaze me. No matter how much I tried to find ulterior motives it became obvious to me that what they said had to be taken at face value. They were in this to serve Allah and for the glory of Islam to be revealed to future generations.

One man stood out in the region as an example to many. At over ninety years of age he had served his followers for almost seventy years. In all that time it was his practice to rise with the sun and retire to bed shortly after the last prayer of the evening had been completed. During his waking hours his primary focus was to share his knowledge of Islam with those who would hear his words. Despite millions of followers and an international reputation as a genius of Islamic thought and practice, the man lived in a home which in the United States would have been considered barely adequate for human habitation. The recipient of hundreds of thousands of dollars in support, monies were poured into expanding the library and teaching facilities within the compound and setting up other training facilities outside of the leader's region.

As my research continued and I began to spend more time among Islamic leaders and their followers, my respect for their devotion to their religion grew. There is no question that they understand life to be a struggle and Islam to be that which makes it worth living. As time wore on, however, and I began to blend into life among these circles of influence, I became increasingly aware that much of their struggle seemed to be directed against particular nations of the world. Although most of my personal experiences shared with

Muslims within the world of fundamentalist Islam were very positive indeed, the times in which the darker side of their struggle became evident remain disturbing to this day.

Chapter Four

Warning Signs

Entering the world of fundamentalist Islam represented a privilege to me. I arrived as one who genuinely sought to learn from the people of this world. As opportunities presented themselves to undertake participant observation, however, it soon became apparent that not all of what I learned represented benign information of interest only to those within the discipline of cultural anthropology or spiritual insights for my missionary colleagues. Rather, a good bit of the details I gathered seemed more suitable for practitioners of espionage.

The Accidental Spy

As my fieldwork continued and several informants became increasingly open with me, many of my notes began to include details more appropriate to an intelligence report than to an anthropologist's data sheet. Not being connected in any way with the Central Intelligence Agency, and not uncovering any specific, dated threats, I simply began noting the darker findings with the other data I collected, and it soon became a routine part of living out life within the world of fundamentalist Islam. As months turned into years, however, and international events unfolded which further aggravated relations between the West and Muslims around the world, the information I gathered became increasingly troubling.

I mentioned in the previous chapter that many with whom I worked treated me as something of an anomaly. The fact that my life did not fit with their picture of what Americans were like meant to many that while I was undeniably from the United States, I was certainly not of it. Perhaps, in their minds, this is why I had chosen to live among them. Though I never sought to give such an impression, it was very clear that many informants with whom I worked felt at ease when speaking about aspects of the West which they felt were despicable.

It should be made clear that I consider myself to be very much a patriot. Living overseas for years in settings in which even the basics of democracy and freedom were often absent tends to endear one all the more to the principles upon which the United States is founded. At least this is true of my situation. I often found myself defending the reputation of my home country against all manner of misrepresentation and exaggeration. At other times I would let points made in conversations between others go unchallenged in order to understand the thinking of those speaking. When asked directly, however, I would always attempt to explain the situation in question from the perspective of the United States, even when doing so was uncomfortable.

This was not too difficult for me when I lived in these areas during the presidencies of Ronald Reagan and George Bush. The actions taken by these presidents seemed quite easy to explain, and even defend, most of the time. This was true even when such actions proved to be very unpopular among Muslims. This was not the case, however, after Bill Clinton became president. It was often pointed out to me that President Clinton claimed to be a true follower of Christ. The reality that he was often embroiled in one or another scandal for allegedly acting in a grossly immoral or dishonest manner did very real harm to the reputation of the United States among Muslims. World events which were judged to represent western aggression against Islam, coupled with the Clinton presidency, gave rise to increasing hostility toward the West during the 1990s. This progression became very apparent in many ways.

In the same way in which conversations with Muslims revealed a growing hostility toward the West in general, and the United States in particular, publications such as books and newspapers became increasingly critical of the western world and the super power which was understood to be its leader. Newspaper stories outlining the sinful nature of the United States and its leader were common, as were attacks on the Christian faith. I vividly recall picking up a book offered for sale which compared the Bible in its present form to a roll of toilet paper. As reports and writings filtered down through the masses and gross exaggerations of incidents which were bad enough when understood as they actually happened became commonplace, a very discernable tendency toward growing militancy within Islam became apparent. Questions which had once been asked in a spirit of curiosity gave way to condemnations of what was understood to be reality.

One of the aspects of living within the world of Islam which serves as a frequent reminder of the religious nature of the society is the call to prayer. Five times a day beginning just after sunrise, the call reminds the faithful of their duties to Allah as practiced by Muhammad. As the call pounds forth from public address speakers high atop the mosque's minaret, all within earshot are reminded of the greatness and oneness of Allah and the role of Muhammad as his Prophet. "Come to prayer, come to success," the message continues. And so they come. Whether in the privacy of their homes or together in the mosque they bow in reverence to Allah. Never having lived outside of the range of the call to prayer during my time in such lands, it becomes a very steady part of daily life.

On Fridays, around noontime, the call is for all men to gather at the mosque to worship together and hear encouragement from one who is rightly guided. Responding in faith, those in attendance are treated to what might be considered the equivalent of the weekly sermon offered in the churches of Christendom. I often took advantage of these times to take a quiet stroll through the mostly empty streets, careful not to be a distraction to anyone. For years, the themes overheard included encouragement in the faith and the idea that Muslims must work together despite any differences which may occur. The faithful are often reminded that although their primary allegiance may well be to the community of faith, or "Ummah," within their local area, they must never forget that they are part of the larger Ummah Islam which encompasses the worldwide community of Muslims. Always an important element in Islamic thought, the Ummah Islam became an increasingly visualized and experienced entity as a common enemy became increasingly well defined.

During the latter 1990s the themes heard during my Friday walks began to focus more and more on the West and how Muslims must not allow globalization to interfere with their devotion to Allah. "Do not walk in the sinful path of America," one might hear in the language of the region as a voice over the public address speaker of yet another mosque is heard to say "We must unite with all Muslims against the sinful West."

As these themes became more and more prevalent, and the message that the West has become an active enemy of Islam echoed throughout the Muslim world, conversations began to focus on how the faithful should respond. Warning signs that rhetoric was giving way to action became apparent as organizations began to arise whose sole purpose was to fight against westerners and those within Islamic nations who were believed to be "puppets" of western governments.

A Front Row Seat

The themes and rally cries of these groups became vividly apparent on a particular day. I had been invited by a prominent Islamic leader to attend the anniversary of the founding of an organization to which he belonged. Knowing that the gathering was not open to outsiders, I was thrilled to have an invitation. I looked forward with great anticipation to what I might learn.

Approaching to within several miles of the area, I was surprised to see crowds as I have never seen before. I was aware that the membership of the organization numbered in the millions, yet certainly did not expect that a good percentage of them would be in attendance. I learned that the people I met on the way had traveled for days to be there, and that it would be one of the largest gatherings of its kind that could be remembered.

After much time and great effort, I arrived at the home of the man who had invited me. The now familiar circle of influential men were already gathered around the room, and great anticipation filled the air. Everyone in attendance seemed awed by the unbelievable size of the crowds, and an atmosphere of intensity few had ever experienced permeated the scene.

I was handed a written invitation just in case I happened to be questioned by someone. It was made out to a man whose name I did not recognize, someone who clearly "belonged" within this group of devoted insiders. I was then escorted to one of the waiting cars. There were several vehicles lined up to receive those who were undoubtedly very prominent men. Many I knew, but there were several whom I did not recognize. The convoy made its way at length through crowds the likes of which I had never seen. The multitudes parted as police vehicles led the way with sirens blaring.

After considerable time the car in which I had been riding

came to a stop in the middle of what can only be described as a sea of humanity. A platform with an enormous public address system had been set up in the middle of a wide field. The men in the first few cars made their way to the stage. The man who had invited me explained that he must also sit on the platform, and that it would be better if I sat in one of the first few rows. I took my place and settled in. The area around us was covered by a long expanse of poles topped with material which kept the hot sun from burning those sheltered underneath. As I surveyed the scene I noted that people had crowded around for as far as I could see. Most were outside the shaded area, at the mercy of the sun. They seemed not even to notice this fact.

When introductions were made I was surprised to hear that several men who were on the platform were visitors from far outside the area. In fact, I believe a few were from outside the region altogether. This accounts for the reason that I had not recognized them earlier. One by one the honored guests were invited to address the assembled crowd. As the speeches began, the theme of the day quickly became apparent. It would be a long and detailed indictment of the West, particularly the United States, and encouragement for all true Muslims to join in the struggle against these enemies of Islam. In addition to condemnations aimed at political views held by the West, attacks on Christianity and issues concerning the general lack of morality in the United States were common. "And did you realize," one man shouted in anger, "that when we send our young Muslim men to the USA for university studies they are forced to convert to Christianity." This really whipped the crowd into a state of frenzied agitation. Another continued "We have been able to determine that now over fifty percent of the marriages in the USA are between members of the same sex." This elaborate condemnation of the United States went on for a very long period of time.

Looking around at the enormous crowd, now yelling at what had become a deafening level, I wondered what would happen if someone suddenly pointed me out as an American. Not wanting to dwell on the possibilities I continued listening to the barrage of insults aimed at my countrymen. I had come, after all, to learn. And what I was learning was very disturbing indeed. The United States had been transformed in the period of a few years from a nation which sought to rid the world of unbelief in the form of Communism to an evil entity, an intensely hated enemy of Islam.

It became very apparent to me that day that militant Islam was becoming increasingly organized. Although the large organizations with which I had worked carefully distanced themselves from the most extreme rhetoric, it was beginning to become evident that a loose collection of highly organized groups were feeling each other out for the possibility of some sort of common association.

For some time rumors of this or that leader joining in with "those who would take action" circulated. It seemed that no one really knew what was happening at the highest levels, but that everyone knew that something was happening, and that things were not what they had once been. It was as if a great storm was brewing and that clouds were gathering, yet no one knew what would happen or when the rain would actually begin to fall.

A Chilling Conversation

The extraordinary opportunities I had been given through association with Ahmed, Abdul, and then a host of others over time made it possible for me to learn much of that which my fieldwork was designed to uncover. Through these circles of influence among which I had grown comfortable, however, I had been given hints of a new, more militant, international element within Islam which was taking shape. The possibility of learning more about this covert entity was very intriguing.

The levels at which I had been working were very significant within the world of Islam. They included most of the direct leadership of the masses. As has been made clear previously, the leaders with whom I worked were responsible for many millions of devoted followers. It was these men whom I had come to study. Over the years I had learned a great deal about their world and about the way they think. Yet I had also learned that there existed above them a very small number of individuals from various nations who operated on a higher level. Whereas the men I had been living among are known as learned men of wisdom, this other level is home to those who have a very different agenda. They are understood to be men of action.

Details about this other level were few, and after some time it became apparent to me that this was the case because those with whom I associated were not privileged to the more clandestine information which I now sought. I wondered what the chances were of an insider from this higher echelon of international, militant Islam suddenly appearing in my life as Ahmed and Abdul had. Not very good, I reasoned.

As I thought back about all those I had met over time who were native to these lands, I suddenly recalled someone whom I had not seen in over ten years. I had met him very much by chance while on a trip to Washington, DC, back in 1986. I recalled how he had been sent by the government of his nation to attend graduate school in the United States as part of his very quick upward climb within the realms of power. It turns out that Hasan, as we shall refer to my friend, had a keen interest in sightseeing. He had traveled to the capital of the United States because he only had one final semester before returning to his home country. His one regret was that he would not be able to see New York City before he left, as he knew no one there and could not afford the hotels. After spending several afternoons together in Washington, DC, I explained to Hasan that I lived close enough to New York City to visit, and I offered to have him and his family stay with me at my home just before return-ing to his home country later that year. The fact that I had made his day was very obvious.

When it came time for the visit, Hasan showed up with his wife, children, and several of his friends. Although I was a bit surprised at the size of the entourage, we finally managed to travel to New York City and see the sights. He was most impressed, as I recall, with the Statue of Liberty and the World Trade Center. After returning to my home Hasan made a great show of thanking me for my outstanding hos-pitality and begging me to visit him at his home someday when I traveled to his country.

And so it came to be that ten years later I dug through my

pile of old business cards and found Hasan's name. I began making a few phone calls to the capital and found that he worked at the very highest level within the country's leadership. Not knowing what would become of it I traveled to the capital, caught a taxi, and asked the driver to take me to the address which I had been given. "You must know someone very important to want to go there," he suggested.

It should be made clear at this point that relationships with people from within the Islamic world are somewhat different from those made between westerners. Once a relationship has been established and solidified through shared experiences, time has little bearing on the depth of the friendship. It is as if it has become an entity unto itself and can be reestablished at any moment without having to explain the long period of time which may have elapsed between visits. There also exists something of an "I owe you" balance which is well understood and never forgotten. Hospitality having been extended, the opportunity to repay it is very much desired. It was with the reality of this situation subconsciously tucked away that I approached the building which housed many of the nation's "best and brightest" minds.

Entering the highly-polished reception area I was immediately confronted by armed security men who sternly requested my credentials. It was an awkward moment. For all they knew I was a foreign diplomat of whose visit they had not been made aware, and so they dare not be too aggressive. On the other hand I may have been a foreigner seeking revenge on one of the country's leaders for some quasi-official military action which resulted in the premature death of a relative, and so a degree of vigilance was certainly in order. The intensity evident on their faces relaxed a bit as I greeted them in their own language and explained that I was an old friend of Hasan, and that I had simply stopped in for an unannounced visit. I was offered a seat as calls were placed to verify my story. After some time the now very polite guards presented me with a security pass and led me to an elevator with instructions on how to locate Hasan. Arriving at the correct floor I was greeted by a receptionist and offered a seat in a plush room which appeared to be used for private meetings.

The look on Hasan's face surprised me as he entered the room alone. I had expected a joyful reunion, and yet his face looked troubled, or perhaps sad. The reason for this became clear as he began to speak. He explained that one of his immediate family members who had spent those wonderful days with us in New York City had died just months after Hasan and his family returned to their home country. Before passing away, she recalled their time in New York, noting that it had been among the highlights of her life. Our time together in the distant past, I now realized, meant a great deal more to Hasan than I had known, and my unexpected visit had apparently brought back the painful memory of the death of his close relative. It seemed also to expand the sense of obligation Hasan felt for the hospitality which had meant so much to his loved one. As I would soon find out, however, Hasan's mind was racing through far more than simply what had taken place in the past.

The conversation surrounding our reunion began to wind down, and Hasan remained silent for several moments.

Seemingly lost in deep thought, he appeared to be weighing various important options. Apparently making up his mind, Hasan explained that he had several hours of work which must be completed before we could travel together to his home where we would have a wonderful time. In a move that surprises me to this day Hasan then ushered me into the office of the leader to whom he was the right-hand-man. Noting that the man was abroad on a diplomatic mission Hasan calmly suggested that I spend the few hours here in this comfortable office and made a point of suggesting that I read whatever caught my attention. As he left Hasan motioned to a glass-enclosed bookcase and cabinet close beside the leader's desk, noting that the material they held might be of interest.

I have no doubt that one trained in the arts of espionage would have instantly recognized the moment for what it was. A sometimes naive and always intensely private person myself, however, I had no clue why Hasan would suggest that I spend hours looking into what were obviously the private papers of one of the nation's most powerful men. Surveying the well-appointed, two-room office I confined myself to reading books concerning foreign policy issues. I found them in an open-shelf bookcase in the middle of the second room. I then settled in for what I thought would be a long wait.

Sooner than I had anticipated Hasan appeared at the door announcing that we should leave. Once outside of the building we began to discuss what I had been able to read. Obviously surprised that I had limited myself to foreign policy issues, Hasan grew quiet. He finally spoke. "Look," he began, "I am not the person you knew ten years ago. You need to understand that I am now political." In the ensuing discussion it became very clear that by "political," Hasan meant that he was part of the leadership of a loose association of militant Islamic groups. It was also evident that he was concerned with the direction in which this entity was headed, and that he wanted me to understand what was happening.

Looking back on that day, I have a strong sense that my visit brought back vivid memories for Hasan of the enjoyable experiences he had in the United States during his graduate studies. After returning home and climbing the ladder of success among his own people Hasan had become closely associated with men who were prime movers within the upper echelons of international, militant Islam. As the trusted right-hand-man of one of the nation's most powerful political, and aggressively Islamic leaders, Hasan had been privy to the plans and schemes of this clandestine association of radical men from various parts of the Islamic world. Having been carried along within this culture of militancy for some ten years, Hasan now seemed to have been taking advantage of an opportunity to allow a representative of the enemy to learn what was being planned.

To this day I am not certain what motivated Hasan to take this course of action. Was it guilt? Was it a sense of responsibility to a nation that had been very good to him during his days as a graduate student? Did it concern the sense of obligation he felt to repay my hospitality of long ago? Or perhaps it had something to do with the member of his family who had spoken so well of the United States just before succumbing to a fatal illness. As Hasan himself died of the same disease a year or so after our meeting, I will never know for sure. Whatever the reason, however, Hasan saw my visit as his chance to make known what had been a closely guarded secret. The hours alone in that plush office had been an opportunity for me to discover first-hand what was being planned. To see in the leader's own hand-written journals and sketchpads the agenda which had been set in motion. Having failed to grasp the opportunity, Hasan apparently felt he had no alternative but to paint out the larger picture for me so there would be no misunderstanding just how serious the situation had become.

The conversation which followed had a chilling tone. In exhaustive detail, Hasan made clear the reasons why the West has become a target for destruction. He also outlined the strategic plan regarding how this objective will be accomplished. At any other time and place the lecture might have been dismissed as the conspiracy theory of a troubled mind. As Hasan carefully explained the circumstances, however, missing pieces to the thousand-piece puzzle on which I had been working for some time began to fall into place. By the time he finished, I sat staring at a completed blueprint that seemed to come straight from hell.

Apocalypse Now

Over the next few years I was busy teaching within the country. I kept to myself the information that Hasan had shared. As one trained to critically test any propositional theory, I waited to see if several key pieces of the puzzle would fall into place as suggested by Hasan. Without exception the scenario began to unfold exactly as it had been explained to me. The unmistakable pattern remained vividly apparent, and I found myself being able to predict the next moves. It would have been a thrilling hobby had it not been for the fact that thousands of lives were being lost in the process.

Along with my wife and children, I returned to the United States during the summer of 2001 for an extended furlough. After doing so I considered the question of how I could best share with others the troubling information I had discovered. There was no question in my mind that militant Islam would eventually represent the greatest challenge to western civilization since the fall of the Soviet Union. Sharing such concerns, however, with Americans whose greatest challenge at that time seemed to be protecting their investment portfolios in a slowing economy seemed like an exercise in futility. I must admit that life back in the "land of the free and the home of the brave" has a way of making troubles common to those living in distant lands seem so much less real. It is as if a security shield existed around the United States that created a zone of invincibility.

During my first few months back life within the zone continued as it always had. The unspoken optimism that life would progress toward a great day in the future when all Americans could enjoy the pursuit of happiness held forth as an ideal within the Declaration of Independence remained unchallenged. Despite such optimism, I felt I had a responsibility to share with Americans what I had learned. I genuinely felt that Hasan would have wished this as well. This being the case I decided to use my six-month sabbatical to write a novel in which a fictional sequence of events would illustrate the threat which I had come to understand. On the morning of September 11, 2001, I was working on plot lines in the quiet corner of the public library in town when I heard a radio. It belonged to a research librarian. The volume had been turned up so that those in the library could follow an important news story.

As events of the morning became clear I watched the faces of those around me. I recognized the look of horror well. I had seen it many times during my years overseas. I realized at that moment that our shield of invincibility had been penetrated, and that more pieces of the puzzle had been snapped into place by those orchestrating the agenda that had been so carefully explained to me several years before.

Work on what I hope would have been an excellent novel ended that day. How I wish the world in which such events were relegated to the realm of fiction still existed.

The remainder of this work outlines the realities we now face and addresses many fundamental misunderstandings which have been widely accepted as truth. For readers not wishing to leave the innocence which characterized life within the zone of invincibility, I recommend this book be placed on a dusty shelf at this point. There is a certain degree of solace that can be enjoyed within the realm of benevolent misinterpretation. To those who wish to contemplate the realities of the world in which we now live, however, I humbly offer this work in hopes that it may answer several of the questions few dare to ask. For in the new world since the morning of September 11, 2001, it seems to me that courage can best be served through a deeper understanding of those who count themselves our mortal enemies.

Chapter Five

A Question of Interpretation

In order to fully comprehend the strategy aimed at destroying western civilization, it is vitally important to gain a deeper understanding of those who have so carefully crafted it. This is especially so in a day and age in which quick answers to complex issues are so authoritatively issued and readily accepted.

Misconceptions

With western media sources as his only guide, one might be tempted to consider those who have been labeled "our new enemies" as a rag-tag group of Arab terrorists cowering in the dark recesses of a cave in some distant desert region. Fervently praying to Allah that the special forces sent to rout them out would fail, it will be just a matter of time before they are all captured and punished for their crimes against humanity. As pleasant as it would be to live in such a well-ordered world, these views represent a dangerously absurd underestimation of those who seek our destruction. In a similar way the general public has been given the impression that the men responsible for what took place on September 11, 2001, and other terrorist activities are crazed lunatics who represent the embodiment of evil. Like Hitler and other villains of history they have been characterized as psychologically unstable men driven by hatred and demonic visions of power.

When people learn that I have spent years working closely with what they call "fanatical Muslims" in their "terrorist training camps" and have spent considerable time with their leaders, more than anything else they want to know what these people are really like. What do they believe? What do they want? How can they be such beasts? These are questions I often hear. Christians are especially interested in gaining an understanding of how all this fits in with faith. Many have a strong desire to understand why Muslims, many of whom speak of their faith as a peace-loving religion, would suddenly target the West for destruction.

It is unfortunate that much of what Americans view and read through the news media is based on conclusions drawn from profound misunderstandings. The truth is that those who count themselves our enemies represent vast, well organized numbers, that far from being characterized by insanity their leaders are brilliant, and that while we have just begun to see tangible evidence of their hatred for us, the animosity has been simmering for centuries.

Before any intelligent discussion concerning the matter at hand continues it is essential to identify just who it is that has chosen to target western civilization in general, and the United States in particular, for destruction. The United States government and most media sources have chosen the term "terrorists" to identify those they call "America's new enemies." This is an unfortunate choice since the terminology tends to significantly confuse the matter. Indeed, we are given daily updates through countless sources concerning how American troops are fairing in our "War on Terrorism." In order to understand what took place on September 11, 2001, what is taking place today, and what will happen in the future, it is vital to recognize that our enemies identify themselves as Muslims serving the cause of Allah.

Imagine the absurdity of characterizing America's involvement in Vietnam as the "War on Insurgency," and simply referring to those who sought to conquer South Vietnam as "subversives." While one might argue that the characterization is accurate in a limited and literal sense, it hardly speaks to the larger issues of French colonialism, Communism, and the Domino Theory to name just a few. In the same way, characterizing the Muslims who have targeted the West for destruction as terrorists, however politically expedient such terminology might be, trivializes the larger issues involved.

Dividing Lines

In a previous chapter I suggested that for the purposes of this discussion Muslims should be understood as belonging to either cultural, Quranic, or militant Islam. I explained that the point of demarcation between cultural and Quranic Islam involves the foundation on which one's philosophical out-look, or cultural world-view, is built. For the cultural Muslim the values and practices common among the society into which he or she was born or now lives represents this foun-dation. The fact that many Islamic societies are extremely conservative and may even operate to a large degree on Quranic principles should not confuse the issue. We are con-cerned here with individuals and the manner in which they live out their faith. No matter how conservative the society to which they belong, cultural Muslims primarily adhere to social norms rather than specific revelation. Looking at the world of Islam as a whole, I believe my Muslim friends would argue that the vast majority of Muslims should be understood as belonging to this category. In short, they are Muslims because they were born into Islam.

For those within the category of Quranic Islam, however, cultural considerations take a back seat to the explicit teach-ings of the Quran and Hadith. At some point in the life of a Quranic Muslim, he or she embraced the faith as his or her own. I suppose to make the distinction clear to those within the western world it would be accurate to say that whereas those within cultural Islam are Muslims because they were born into Islam, Quranic Islam is home to Muslims who have been "born again" into what they understand to be true Islam.

Much like evangelical Christians, Quranic Muslims seldom attempt to live out their faith alone. They generally "belong" to a group of like-minded individuals who have chosen the same path of obedience to what they understand to be God's revealed truth. It is inevitable that such groups will tend to focus on various issues of faith. Whereas in Christianity this reality has led to denominations, within Quranic Islam it has led to the formation of various organizations.

Just as is true within the realms of Christianity, such institutions are generally led by those who have spent many years in formal "theological" training. At the risk of offending my fellow believers, I would argue that the leadership of significant organizations within the realm of Quranic Islam take their roles a bit more seriously than do their counterparts in Christianity. As evidence I would cite the fact that it is not unusual to find men in this capacity who have memorized the entire Quran word for word. I have yet to meet a pastor or teacher within Christendom who can claim to have memorized even the New Testament. This unusual degree of commitment to Islam and to their fellow Muslims tends to filter down to the membership of these organizations.

The exact role played by leaders of Quranic Islam varies from one organization to another. Such issues depend greatly on factors such as historical development, geographical location, and the school of Islamic jurisprudence to which the men adhere. In most cases, however, the leadership of such organizations are highly respected men whose decisions are given tremendous weight by the members of the organization in question. This brings us to the point of demarcation between the categories of Quranic and militant Islam.

As one undertakes a careful study of the Quran several recurring themes become evident. One such theme involves the manner in which those who follow Islam constitute a brotherhood which has been set apart from the rest of mankind. Known as the Ummah Islam in Arabic, all true believers are members of this "community" who have received the truth.

To a far greater degree than most individuals from the western world can understand, the group mentality and sense of inclusion are profoundly important aspects of Islam. Beginning as a small band of believers held together through common submission to the revelations received by Muhammad in the early 7th century AD, Islam has grown to include well over a billion followers. Despite the numbers involved, a very tangible insular mentality remains. It is as if the Ummah were an island of faith within an ocean of unbelief. Added to this is the perception that the ocean would very much like to once and for all submerge the island beneath its relentless waves.

Just as Muhammad himself was born into a tribal society given to warfare and was a hunted man for much of his adult life, a very discernable view of the Ummah as a persecuted minority is noticeable in the Quran. The following verse demonstrates this point:

> When you journey throughout the land it is not a sin if you need to perform your prayers in haste because you fear an attack from unbelievers, for surely the infidels are your enemies. When you are among them and begin the prayer service, let some stand with you keeping their weapons ready. After they have completed their prayers, let them go to the rear and the next group may come in turn, being careful to be armed as well. For the

unbelievers would take any opportunity to find you off your guard so they may suddenly attack you. It is not a sin if you have to put aside your weapons due to rain or an illness, yet always be on your guard. Allah has surely prepared a humiliating punishment for the infidels. (author's interpretation of 4:101-102).

In this and many other passages the theme of the Ummah as a united people targeted for destruction by non-Muslims is abundantly clear. This perception remains deeply ingrained within Islamic culture to this day. Even in geographic regions where Muslims constitute almost 100% of the population, the threat is clearly understood to be just outside the area under Islamic control. The importance of understanding this mindset within Islamic culture cannot be overemphasized.

Understanding themselves to be a threatened people like all others within the Ummah, Quranic Muslims are particularly sensitive to the defense of their faith. This is understandable for several reasons. First, it is they who follow Islam most closely, who seek on a daily basis to apply the teachings of the Quran to their lives. With this in mind it is obviously Quranic Muslims who have the highest stake in ensuring the continuance of traditional Islam. In addition, as a scholarly people, Quranic Muslims have carefully studied history and understand that Islamic civilization has been threatened many times since its inception. This was especially the case during the Age of Colonialism in which many Islamic lands were ruled by western powers. This situation is still fresh in the minds of Quranic Muslims, and they have no wish to return to such times.

During times when the Ummah is not directly threatened, Quranic Muslims seek to "defend the faith" through living it as purely as possible. This includes bringing glory to Allah by fulfilling the obligation to spread the message of Islam throughout the world by peaceful means. Many feel that if outsiders could just see Muslims live out their faith within an Islamic society and be exposed to the message of the Quran, that much of the world would embrace Islam as the only genuine path to God.

In addition to focusing on individual and group purity, many Quranic Muslims are politically active in an effort to encourage their countrymen to adopt forms of government based more on Quranic principles than on models left by former colonial powers. The idea is that if predominantly Islamic nations would operate on Quranic principles, and the citizens within them would live their lives based on Quranic teachings, other nations would see the glory of Islam and many would come to faith.

The realization that western models of democratic government are making inroads into Islamic lands is particularly troubling to many of these men. It is understood that in the West democracy has been elevated to the status of a faith, and that tremendous pressure is placed on developing nations to adopt its fundamental tenants. A major concern is that the core doctrine of this "western philosophy" ensures that power to govern rests with the common man, or "the people." It is pointed out that to the degree that the people are misled, government based on such a system is open to manipulation and corruption. A related concern is that as misguided citizens become increasingly immoral and concerned only with their individual rights and privileges, the very fabric uniting them will decay, and the nation itself will eventually succumb to ruin. In contrast, it is felt that when power rests in the hands of leaders who govern according to Quranic principles and apply the laws of Islamic jurisprudence, the people of such a rightly-guided nation will continually grow in righteousness and prosperity.

The struggle to continually live according to the revealed will of Allah in a corrupt world accounts for the efforts of most within Quranic Islam. The journey toward individual adherence to the faith, the encouragement of others to grow in their knowledge of the truth, and the effort to reform one's nation and eventually the world through peaceful means represents the desires and life efforts of many of the men with whom I have worked over the years. I can honestly say that, to a man, these individuals are model citizens living honorable lives for what they perceive to be righteous ends. The world would be a far better place were it home to more men such as these.

How, then, does one account for all the bloodshed associated with Islam over the centuries? The line of demarcation between Quranic and militant Islam represents a tenuous, fluid barrier which we misunderstand at our peril.

Upon this tenuous dividing line sit the leaders of Quranic Islam. These men, perhaps numbering just a few thousand worldwide, are faced with an important question of interpretation. It should be remembered that inherent within Islam is the sense that the Ummah must continually be on guard from outside threats, and that as long as no direct threat exists to Islamic civilization in general or the Ummah in particular, Quranic Muslims generally should focus on purity and the peaceful spread of the faith.

The question that begs interpretation is this: To what degree is the Ummah or Islamic civilization under direct attack? The importance of this question cannot be overemphasized, for the answer determines on which side of the militant fence the leader and his followers fall. Those who sense no direct threat to Islam remain Quranic Muslims, while those who perceive a clear attack initiated by infidels generally seek to fulfill their Quranic duty to enter the fray and defend the faith, thus joining the ranks of militant Islam. Since many of the leaders perched upon the fence between Quranic and militant Islam represent followings that number in the many thousands, and some in millions, interpretation of this all-important question has tremendous implications.

Chapter Six

Militant Islam

It has often been said that Islam is a religion of peace. It has even been suggested by some that in the Arabic language the word Islam, usually translated "submission," can also refer to the concept of nonviolence. Given these arguments, why has Islam been associated for centuries, and especially recently, with war and bloodshed? Why is the cry "Allah akbar," or "God is greater" so often heard just before mass destruction and tremendous loss of life is experienced? The answer to these questions is of vital importance if the citizens of western civilization desire to understand those who have targeted them for destruction.

Definitions

As suggested in the previous chapter, the question of how violence becomes associated with Islam involves an important point of interpretation. Quranic teachings make it very clear that Muslims are not to attempt to spread their faith by force and are not to be initiators of war. It is just as clear, however, that when the Ummah is under attack, it is the responsibility of every true Muslim to defend it. Along with many other passages, the following verses make this point clear:

> Fight in the way of Allah those who fight you, but do not be the aggressor, for Allah is not pleased with aggressors. Kill them wherever you may find them, and expel them from where they cast you out, for oppression is worse than slaughter. But do not make war by the Holy Mosque, unless you are attacked there, in this case slay them, for such is the reward of infidels. But if they relent, Allah is forgiving and most merciful. Make war with them until there is no more oppression, and religion is for Allah. But if they cease fighting, let there be no hostilities except with the oppressors (author's interpretation of 2:191-193).

Perhaps no other excerpt from a religious text has been responsible for more bloodshed than the verses quoted above. It is not difficult to see why the passage is read in so many different ways by various leaders. For the reader inclined toward peace, the message is clear: Muslims are not to initiate conflicts, and as soon as direct hostilities end peace is to be sought at all cost. Just as understandably, however, those who are of a more bellicose nature read just the opposite: Muslims must fight all non-Muslims until Islam dominates the world and infidels are brought under submission.

I suppose it is accurate to say that most scholars fall somewhere between these two extreme views. That is, it is generally understood that Muslims are commanded to defend Islam when it is under attack and should do so until the threat to the Ummah has ended. With this in mind the all-important question open for interpretation concerns exactly what it is that constitutes a threat to Islam. For the purposes of this discussion, the answer to this question divides cultural and Quranic Islam from militant Islam. In order to clarify the distinction, I propose the following as a working definition of militant Islam:

> Militant Islam refers to that portion of the Islamic Ummah which is actively engaged in defending the faith by means of armed conflict and/or other strategic efforts aimed at the destruction or subjugation of non-Muslims who are understood to constitute a threat to Islamic populations in particular, or Islamic civilization in general.

It must be understood that the "portion of the Islamic Ummah" that may be considered militant by the above definition may increase or decrease at particular times and in certain places as threats to Islam come and go. During periods when a significant portion of the Ummah is clearly threatened, for example, the ranks of militant Islam may swell drastically, whereas in times when no clear threat is perceived the vast majority of Muslims concern themselves with the peaceful pursuits of everyday life.

There have been many historical situations in which Muslim populations have come under direct attack and all involved have had to respond. Regardless of whether one might have been a cultural, Quranic, or militant Muslim prior to the attack, many will respond by taking up arms to defend the Ummah. This is the situation we see today between Israel and Palestine, and to some degree it can serve as a microcosm representing the wider discussion concerning the various categories of Islam to which we have been referring.

The Palestinians fighting Israel are often referred to by the media as militant Muslims. On one hand, using this same logic, it would be necessary to refer to anyone who seeks to defend his or her homeland as militant. Kuwaitis, then, who sought to defend their land from the advances of Saddam Hussein in 1990 should have been termed militant Muslims, and the coalition forces who fought in the Gulf War must then be understood as having supported, to at least some degree, the cause of militant Islam. Many in the pro-Israeli West who use this term referring to Palestinians tend to do so in a derogatory manner, and at times seem to choose it to justify further military action against the Palestinians. Considering the potential consequences of its misuse, the term "militant" when applied to Muslims or Islam in this work will be limited to the meaning outlined above.

The fact is that many Palestinians see themselves more as patriots than holy warriors. In a strict sense many Palestinians do not fit our definition of militant Islam since their goal is political autonomy rather than the destruction or subjugation of Israel. It is not difficult to understand, however, that within an atmosphere like the one surrounding the

Israeli-Palestinian conflict, the percentage of Muslims who choose the path of militancy tends to rise as months or years pass and no clear resolution becomes apparent. As hostilities escalate and what may be considered acts of atrocity increase from both directions, what began for some Palestinians as a struggle for increased independence may eventually turn into the desire to see Israel destroyed. In such circumstances the ranks of militant organizations swell, and as time goes on a new generation of truly militant Muslims comes of age. Those who otherwise may have been cultural or Quranic Muslims, as a consequence of the hostilities enter the militant "portion" of the Ummah, and generally grow in their religious and political devotion to Islam.

The same principles are in operation on a much larger scale for those living outside the immediate area of the Israeli-Palestinian and other such zones of armed conflict. As will be discussed in a later chapter, the threats for most of the Islamic world over the past few generations have been of a far more comprehensive and pervasive nature than the border disputes that currently serve to push many Palestinians toward militancy.

The important point to understand here is that militant Islam is by no means limited to areas where armed conflict makes the television news on a nightly basis. The truth is that militant Islam has been quietly growing for several generations, relatively unnoticed by those in the West, including those responsible for guarding against large-scale national security threats. There are now organizations scattered throughout the world which are home to vast numbers of individuals who have targeted the West in general and the

United States in particular for destruction or subjugation. It is remarkable to understand the degree to which this phenomena has taken place seemingly outside of the attention of western intelligence communities.

A very unnerving fact is that the momentum over the past twenty years or so has been aggressively moving toward Islamic militancy. Attempts to share these concerns with those in the West have generally fallen on deaf ears. Before September 11, 2001, one could hardly get anyone to take the issue of Islamic militancy seriously, let alone understand it as a threat to national and international security. Even since the attacks on New York and Washington it seems that every effort is being made to argue that those responsible were not real Muslims, but were a small band of fanatical terrorists hiding out in desert caves. When governments and media sources confuse militant Islam with terrorist groups in this way, they do so at our peril. Whereas terrorist networks generally refer to relatively small splinter groups, it must be understood that militant Islam already involves millions and has the very real potential of involving hundreds of millions of religious warriors bent on our destruction.

As international events continue to unfold that cause thinking people to question the "desert cave" paradigm, I am often asked about these men who count themselves our mortal enemies. When friends learn that I have spent many years living among and seeking to understand the worldview of such individuals, I am often asked questions such as: Who are these people? Where do they live? What do they believe? What do they want? Why do they hate us so much, and what are their plans?

Breadth and Depth

Despite the fact that many people in the West still view Islam as a predominantly Middle eastern faith, the truth is that the vast majority of Muslims live in either Africa or the regions of South Asia, Southeast Asia or East Asia. Similarly, the popular view that most Muslims are Arab is completely false. In reality Arabs make up only some 15% of all Muslims alive today. Over the past 1400 or so years, Islam truly has grown to become a global religion with significant representation in almost every nation on earth. It is estimated that in the United States alone there are now between six and nine million Muslims.

It must be pointed out, however, that we are concerned here with militant Islam, not Islam in general. The point that Islam has spread throughout the earth is only made to suggest that it would be relatively simple for members of militant groups to move among and secretly infiltrate peaceful Islamic populations wherever and whenever it might be considered strategically important to do so. Most of the core organizations representing openly militant Islam, however, are to be found in nations such as Egypt, Pakistan, Iran, and Indonesia to name just a few. In these and other large nations where the percentage of the population representing Islam reaches well over ninety percent, militant Islam is bound to be well represented whether openly or in a covert manner. That the actions of militant Islamic groups within such nations reflect negatively on the vast majority of their peace-loving countrymen is both tragically inevitable and, as will be discussed later, an important part of the strategic planning of such groups.

Having understood that militant Islamic groups practice openly in certain parts of the world and more covertly in others, the next question concerns just who is involved in these networks which have chosen to target the West. I find that the answer to this question often surprises those who ask it.

Whether openly or in a more clandestine manner, the fact is that association with militant Islam includes individuals from all walks of life. I have established close friendships with representatives of militant Islam who practice peasant farming and with those at the very highest levels of political leadership. The stereotypical view of turban-clad, bearded men sitting in desert settings holding assault rifles in one hand and a copy of the Quran in the other only serves to reinforce the widely held misconception that those associated with militant Islam are a small group of extremists. To be sure these men are a part of the picture, yet they represent only a very small part. The fact that these "poster children" of militant Islam lead outsiders to feel that fanatics must dominate such circles is much appreciated by the true "movers and shakers" of the phenomena. The truth is that both men and women at all levels of society have a role to play in militant Islam. Regardless of social standing or educational background, the common denominator which tends to set militant Muslims apart generally concerns the view that Islam in general and Muslims in particular have been victimized by the West, and that the time has come for action to be taken so that further damage can be averted and ground lost in the past can be reclaimed. There is no question that such views are becoming increasingly popular as time goes on and globalization continues unabated. As I speak with individuals resident in various parts of the Islamic world, the unanimous conclusion is that Islamic militancy is on the rise in most areas.

Numbers have always been problematic with regard to Islam. Even the total number of Muslims worldwide is a hotly debated subject. The low estimates put the total at some 1.2 billion people, and the higher claims place the figure at almost 2 billion. The best estimates I have seen are at about 1.4 billion. Similarly, the growth rate of Islam is very difficult to get a handle on, yet most agree that Islam represents the fastest growing religion in the world. It has been argued by some that this is due partly to the reality that Muslims tend to have more children on average than non-Muslims. I have seen estimates that suggest that even without conversions, Islam will replace other religions biologically at some point if current demographic trends continue. With such confusion over relatively simple questions, one can imagine why I am hesitant to hazard a guess when asked what percentage of the Ummah represents militant Islamic groups who have targeted the West. The simple answer I give is that even if it reaches only 7%, this represents almost 100 million people. With such numbers in mind it is easy to understand why destroying a network of caves in the hills of Afghanistan hardly addresses the larger problem represented by militant Islam.

Understanding that militant Muslims can be found across the globe, that they represent every social strata, and that the total numbers reach into the millions, many people very much want to understand just what makes them tick. When

I think of the men I worked among for so long, four words come to mind: faith, devotion, vision, and action. A later chapter will deal with the action aspect, and so I will limit this section to addressing the first three descriptive terms.

A People of Faith

It should be recognized that the following information by no means represents an exhaustive work regarding the beliefs associated with the religion of Islam. There are many excellent books on the market dealing with these issues. Rather, after presenting a very short summary of a few Islamic beliefs and practices relevant to this discussion, I will attempt to demonstrate that the positions held and the actions undertaken by militant Muslims should be understood as a natural response to the teachings of Islam as these men have interpreted them.

Before delving into such issues, however, it must be understood that preconceived notions regarding Islam should be set aside. This is especially important for the evangelical Christian reader. If one were to study the beliefs and practices of evangelical Christianity through the Islamic perspective, that is, through the writings of a Muslim scholar, the faith would hardly be recognizable to those who practice it. In the same way, when an evangelical believer approaches the study of Islam through the Christian perspective, or through sources written by Christian scholars, the faith of Islam is hardly recognizable to those who know it.

I have heard sermons, especially since the events of September 11, 2001, in which otherwise excellent Christian scholars have butchered Islam through sloppy research based on secondary sources and hearsay. It seems that in such circumstances the principles of sound research and careful preparation normally given to aspects of the Christian faith did not apply as great minds were turned toward a quick review of aspects having to do with the religion of Islam. The danger of such practices is not only that the evangelical community will be seriously misled, but also that such approaches will seem to verify the arguments of Muslim scholars. For years they have taught that Christianity is based on a far less rigorous standard of academic integrity than is the study of Islam. Having set aside our preconceived notions, then, let us look at a few of the very basic tenets of the religion of Islam.

The Concept of God: Muslims are very quick to point out that the Arabic word for God, Allah, refers to the same Almighty God who is worshiped by Christians and Jews. Millions of Arab and other Christians around the world use this same name for the God of the Bible. Since there is only one Creator, Almighty God, and Master of the Day of Judgment, there is no question that it is the same God we are addressing. This fact notwithstanding, orthodox Muslims and evangelical Christians will agree that our "paths" to that God are mutually exclusive. In other words either the Christian or Muslim will awake on the other side of death and be welcomed into heaven, but not both. It is understood by serious followers of each faith that the stakes involved in this debate are very high indeed.

Islam teaches that the Jewish (Old Testament) and

Christian (New Testament) scriptures were sent from God, and that in their original forms held the truth of Allah. It is taught that had these scriptures not been changed and/or misrepresented over the ages to incorporate false beliefs, their teachings would agree with those of Islam (3:78, 5:13).

Allah is understood within Islam to be the merciful, compassionate creator of all mankind. In fact, Allah loved mankind so much that he sent many prophets to show us how to live in order to please Him. These are the same prophets recognized by Judaism and Christianity. The problem is that Jews and Christians, so it is taught, distorted God's teachings and did not even follow that which they did accept without alteration (5:77-79). For this reason a new, clearer scripture had to be communicated to mankind (5:15-16,48). This accounts for the reason that Muhammad was chosen to receive special revelation from Allah.

The Prophet Muhammad: Born in the city of Mecca on the Arabian Peninsula about the year 570 AD, Muhammad lived among a people who were steeped in polytheistic worship. Muslims believe that in the year 610 Muhammad, while on a spiritual retreat in a cave on Mount Hira, heard the command of an angel to recite that which he would receive. Over the next twenty years Muhammad is believed to have received revelation directly from Allah. Word for word, line for line, Muhammad wrote down what he received. This body of revelation came to be known as the Quran (10:37). The Quran is divided into 114 chapters (sura) and then by many verses.

During his lifetime Muhammad lived the message of the

Quran (46:9) and was recognized as a true messenger of Allah and the last prophet that would serve to lead mankind (33:40). It is very clearly taught, however, that Muhammad was no more than an ordinary man who was chosen by Allah to carry truth to mankind (3:144).

The Message: The Quran is intended to lead mankind on the straight path from darkness to light (5:16, 6:155). The most important teaching in the Quran is the oneness of God (tawhid). All manner of sin that an individual commits may be forgiven, except for the sin of ascribing an equal with Allah (shirk). This is the unpardonable sin of Islam (4:48). According to the Quran, this is the great sin associated with Christianity, that Christians have elevated Christ to the status of God and are thus guilty of polytheism (4:171). Those who persist in this teaching will be damned by God (9:30).

The practical application of the message of Islam may be seen in what has become known as the five pillars of the faith. They are as follows:

1. **The Profession of Faith(shahadah)**

   For one to be considered a Muslim, he or she must proclaim the shahada. It states "I testify that there is no god but Allah, and I testify that Muhammad is the messenger of Allah." Within this short proclamation is held the core doctrine that serves to separate Muslims from infidels.

2. **Prayer(salah)**

   Five times a day Muslims are called to worship

Allah in prayer. After performing a cleansing ritual (wudu), they join other Muslims throughout the world who face Mecca and undertake what has become a prescribed form of ritual prayer.

3. **Giving Alms(zakat)**
   Muslims are commanded by Allah to give a portion of their wealth for, among other causes, the poor, and to promote Islam (2:43,7:156). The generally accepted minimum amount is 2.5% of ones accumulated wealth.

4. **Fasting During the Month of Ramadan(sawm)**
   The Quran teaches that Muslims are to fast during Ramadan, the ninth month of the Islamic calendar (2:183-185). From sunrise to sunset Muslims who are physically able are to abstain from food, drink, and sexual activity for this month-long period. This rigorous spiritual discipline helps Muslims to focus on Allah and to devote themselves wholly to Him.

5. **The Pilgrimage(hajj)**
   If physically and financially capable, all adult Muslims are expected to make a pilgrimage to the holy city of Mecca at least once in their lifetime (2:196, 3:97). Located in present-day Saudi Arabia, Mecca is the city of Muhammad's birth, and the location of the most holy place of worship for Muslims, the Ka'bah. This square structure is believed to have been built by Adam, and later

rebuilt by Abraham and his son Ishmael (2:125).

The Concept of Salvation: Muslims, like Christians, believe in a Day of Judgment. On that day, all who during their lifetime accepted and followed the path revealed to Muhammad will enjoy paradise (3:31,2:25,77:41). Those who denied the Quran and chose not to submit to Allah are not loved by him (3:32), and will inherit hell (2:161, 3:12).

Although Christians are quick to point out that while Christianity is a religion of faith and Islam of works, Muslims consider this argument illogical. Certainly one must have faith, they suggest, to believe that Allah loved mankind so much that he took the trouble to send many prophets to show us how to live. If we choose to live according to these revelations, certainly Allah will be pleased and accept us into paradise. In this sense, Muslims have a similar "assurance" of salvation as that enjoyed by Christians.

The Ummah: The Quran speaks of the Ummah, or worldwide community of Islam, as a community set apart from others in order to be a witness to mankind (2:143). The Ummah is referred to as the best community ever found among mankind, teaching what is right, forbidding what is wrong, rightly believing in Allah, and enjoying success (3:104-110).

An important theme within the Quran concerns the teaching that non-Muslims (infidels, or Kafir) will forever attempt to destroy the Ummah and turn Muslims away from the truth of Islam (2:217, 4:101). Muslims are commanded in very strong terms to defend the Ummah by fighting the infidels who persecute Islam (4:74-76).

Defense of the Faith: As noted above, the Quran is very clear about the fact that Islam, as the true faith, will continually be under attack by infidels. During such times and in such places that attacks occur, Muslims are commanded in no uncertain terms to defend the Ummah. In fact it is clearly taught that those who fight to defend Islam will be richly rewarded (4:74). Just as clearly, it is taught that those who turn their back and do not fight will inherit hell (8:15-16). There is no neutral ground with regard to these issues, either one joins the faithful to fight for Allah, or he supports the enemy who, in reality, is fighting for the cause of Satan (4:76).

I stated above that when called to describe militant Muslims, the word "faith" generally enters my mind. I say this because seldom have I been among a people who are more certain of that which they believe. The teachings of the Quran represent the very words of Allah for these people, and they are accepted without reservation or apology.

A People of Devotion

If devotion is defined as loyal adherence to a person or cause, I can think of few other examples that approach the devotional lives of militant Muslims. One factor that gives them an advantage is that they tend to have relatively little in the way of material distractions. When one thinks of the life of the average westerner, he might imagine a man or woman who puts in the required hours at work, shuttles the kids back and forth to a host of sporting events, enjoys an evening meal, and then settles down in the living room of a comfortable home to enjoy television before retiring for the evening and beginning the entire process all over again. Those who mock this as a hollow lifestyle point out that much of this routine revolves around the necessity of being able to afford what are seen as luxuries by citizens of many non-western nations. In other words, many would consider the lifestyle common to the average westerner as an endless cycle of work and play with little or no time devoted to spiritual concerns.

In contrast, many of the men I know who belong to circles fitting the description of militant or Quranic Islam have sought to incorporate the faith into their daily lives to the highest possible degree. I recall the life of one man in particular. He is a teacher of Islamic theology. After dropping his children off at a religious institution for their schooling, my friend would spend his day teaching large groups of university students how to apply the message of the Quran and Hadith to the many complex issues facing Muslims today. After a full day he would retrieve his children, enjoy time with them reviewing what they had learned that day, and then join a group of men from the neighborhood who would gather on his porch. The group would sit facing one another and talk long into the night about world affairs and how Muslims should respond to various issues. Such men are fond of saying that while westerners have divided life into the sacred and secular, there is no such division within Islam. They joke that whereas the sacred is a one-day-a-week thing for Christians, the secular pursuit of wealth actually dominates the lives of such people. They have a saying that while Christianity is a religion, Islam is a way of life.

Another measure of the devotional lives of such people involves their respect for what they consider to be the Word of God. Not only do they enjoy reading and meditating on the message of the Quran, the ideal in such circles is that it be memorized in its entirety. One of the schools I frequented was attended by roughly one thousand students. After a full day of studies, two hours would be spent in the afternoon six days each week in an effort to memorize the Quran. The ideal was that by the time they graduate at the age of eighteen or so, each student would have been given the chance over his or her twelve years at the school to earn the title of Hafiz, or one who has memorized the Quran. A number of the "best and brightest" achieve this remarkable task. It takes them many hours to recite the book from beginning to end.

A People of Vision

It has been suggested that militant Muslims are numerous and can be found in many parts of the globe, and that their lives tend to be characterized by intense devotion to God as they know Him. To at least some degree, the same can be said about Quranic Muslims. What begins to set them apart, however, concerns a deep sense on the part of militants that something is desperately wrong with the status quo – that Islamic civilization should be more than it is.

The perfect world to these individuals would be one in which the glory of Islam is evident to all. Having been blessed by Allah as the best of all communities, the Ummah should shine in every aspect of advancement and learning.

This world would be home to tremendous centers of worship and education in which Muslims would be free to follow the straight path to heaven and seek to glorify Allah through advanced learning.

It is believed that in such a setting, tremendous progress would be made in medicine, political thought, humanitarian concerns, and in the implementation of just economic practices. In such a world, government and commerce would take a back seat to faith so that corruption and usury aimed at the poor would be eradicated. In this way, men and women would be free to become all that Allah intended. Similarly, children would be free to grow and learn unencumbered by the moral disintegration so prevalent in today's world. The emotional scars that so cripple healthy development today would be replaced by confidence rooted in the security offered by faith in Allah. Characterized by justice and morality, it is felt that this prosperous society based on Islamic principles would thrive like no other in history.

Within this ideal world, those choosing to deny the truth of Islam would be free to follow their own faith without hindrance. Communities of Christians and Jews would be offered protection from persecution, and peace would reign between those who choose to live in peace with Islam. Those who seek to persecute Muslims, however, would be dealt with swiftly and without mercy until any such aggression ceases. It is envisioned that within a relatively short period of time society based on Islamic principles and unencumbered by western dominance would represent a shining civilization unequaled in the history of man. It is suggested that such a moral society characterized by advancement and prosperity would surely serve to draw all men closer to the will of Allah as revealed in the Quran, thus fulfilling an important part of why Muhammad was chosen as a messenger so many centuries ago.

When certain thinkers within the ranks of militant Islam contemplate such possibilities, and how they could be realized if the vision were only taken seriously by more Muslims, the strong desire to take steps toward initiating such a glorious age is overpowering. This righteous yearning is made all the more intense when it is remembered that so many Muslims currently live in such dismal conditions and are subject to exploitation from the West. The combination of these realities has led many to plan and undertake what they consider to be heroic actions in the name of Allah.

The realization that militant Muslims represent the portion of the Ummah that has chosen to take up arms to defend Islam, and that they should be viewed as people of faith, devotion, and vision, should serve as a background for a deeper understanding of those who count themselves enemies of the West. An explanation of how militant Muslims view history, especially over the past two generations, will serve to clarify why the momentum toward militancy has been building at such an alarming rate.

Chapter Seven

A Clear and Present Threat

To a degree that would seem unusual to the average adult in the western world, many Muslims have a deep appreciation for, and remarkable familiarity with, world history. This is especially true of the men who represent the learned leadership within Quaranic and militant Islam. For these men, events relating to the history of Islam over the past fourteen centuries have a profound impact on the present, as well as on the establishment of goals for the future.

A History of Persecution

Discussions with learned Muslims about world history often center on the manner in which Muslims throughout the ages have been persecuted by those outside their faith. More pointedly, these men are quick to note that were it not for certain calculated acts on the part of infidels the glorious

Islamic civilization they now envision would already have become a reality. Those who regularly speak of these issues do so with an unusual degree of anger evident in their voices and nonverbal gestures. Clearly, they hold an intense hatred for the infidels who they claim banned together many times over the centuries to purposefully crush Islamic civilization.

Placing the importance of unbiased historical accuracy aside for a moment, it is important to uncover the root causes of this deep-seated animosity if one wishes to understand the motivation that drives militant Muslims to seek the destruction of those they perceive to be a threat to their way of life. From their viewpoint, Islam has been under attack from its inception, and the pace of this persecution has been steadily increasing since the latter part of the 20th century.

A discussion on these points generally begins with the reaction of those who first heard Muhammad's message. When Muhammad sought to share the monotheistic nature of Allah with his people, the Quraish tribe of the Arabian peninsula, his efforts were met with strong opposition.

Steeped in polytheistic practices, the Quraish labeled Muhammad a heretic, and many attempts were made to end his life. Despite such opposition many men and women eventually came to faith in Allah as the one and only God, and the Ummah began to take shape and prosper. Expanding despite strong opposition, within one hundred years of Muhammad's death in 632, Islamic civilization, or perhaps more accurately civilizations, had spread across northern Africa and southern Spain in the west, to parts of India in the east.

Those telling the story light up with enthusiasm when it is pointed out that over the next five hundred years the golden age of Islamic civilization flourished while Europe plunged into what is today known as the Dark Ages. This period was marked by stunning cultural and intellectual achievements as Islamic civilization began to take what is thought to be its rightful place in world history. Important contributions to the fields of math, science, medicine and the establishment of vast trade networks utilizing elaborate credit systems are but a few of the advancements pointed out as originating from this glorious age.

There is no doubt in the minds of those who recount this history that given the opportunity to continue this development, Islamic civilization today would encompass the entire world and would be responsible for achievements beyond the scope of man's current understanding. From the Islamic perspective the fact that this glorious age of Islam was cut short is attributable in large measure to actions taken by representatives of western civilization. Beginning with the Crusades and continuing to current times, militant Muslims angrily recount a long list of historical incidents responsible for the rise of western civilization at the expense of Islamic culture.

To many Muslims the historical period known as the Crusades represents the first comprehensive strategic effort on the part of the Christian West to destroy Islamic civilization. Having, rightly in their minds, made great gains in what we call the Holy Land, Muslims first came under attack after Pope Urban II issued a challenge to Christians in November of 1095 to take Jerusalem back from the Muslims who had come to rule it. Over the next two hundred years or so, Muslims suggest that Christians engaged in all manner of barbaric acts to displace them from this area. The period is remembered today with intense emotion as one of the darkest in Islamic history.

As Islamic culture gained ground in some areas and lost it in others over the ensuing centuries, the next great blows to Islamic civilization are seen as having their roots in the periods of European colonial expansion into South Asia and Southeast Asia, followed by the exploitation made possible by the Industrial Revolution of the mid-18th century. Beginning in Europe with the replacement of manual labor by machines, this revolutionary transformation of production eventually made possible the manufacture of advanced weapons which contributed to the political dominance of western powers over many Islamic lands. The history of how European powers colonized much of the Islamic world is bitterly recounted as yet another means through which western powers sought to replace Islam with Christianity by any means possible. It is suggested that this historic period of overt religious persecution continues in one form or another to this day.

Persecution Intensified

As direct political control of many Islamic lands came to an end through the first half of the 1900s, many Muslims believe that a far more insidious form of persecution began to replace it. Even as Muslims began to regain political leadership among their own people, they soon realized that what was benignly termed "modernization" by westerners was actually a covert attempt by Christian nations to destroy Islamic influence even as it began to reemerge. As Muslim leaders sought access to economic or military aid, conditions aimed at strengthening western values and "democratic principles" were inevitably included. This period of western paternalism is seen as dominating relationships between Islamic and western nations to this day.

As if direct colonization and imperialism followed by paternalistic blackmail were not enough, Muslim thinkers began to notice yet another dangerous trend beginning in the 1980s. What is now known as globalization began to have a profound impact on Islamic nations as communication and information technologies were welcomed by moderate political leaders in many Islamic lands as a means of facilitating development on their own terms. The thinking seems to have been that as Muslims appropriated advanced technologies for their own purposes, Islamic values would be communicated to their own people. Many Islamic leaders now lament the fact that just the opposite has actually taken place.

Anthropologists refer to the process by which values and practices are spread from one culture to another as cultural diffusion. A very powerful phenomenon, this process has been responsible for much of what we consider to be normative in our societies. Rather than every culture having to invent the wheel, for example, when the concept is introduced for the first time to a culture unfamiliar with it, the more familiar yet less practical way of moving heavy objects is quickly replaced by the new practice. In a similar way, when the traditional evening entertainment represented by listening to an elder member of one's family recount heroic deeds of the past in poetic fashion is compared with the universal appeal of color television broadcasting comedy or adventure series produced in the West, Grandpa quickly looses his audience of admiring youth, and subtle cultural practices begin to be adopted by those who eagerly drink in the new form of entertainment. Aided by the now ubiquitous satellite dish, and more recently by the proliferation of the Internet, the vast array of entertainment and information now available has proven an irresistible draw for the masses in many Islamic nations.

Understanding the phenomenal power of cultural diffusion, Islamic leaders have sought to measure the impact that technology has had on their people. Although it is true that certain gains are evident with regards to development and education, the trend toward moral decline and spiritual apathy is unmistakable. For example, men who see it as their responsibility to pass spiritual knowledge on to the next generation decry the fact that whereas in their youth a great deal of time was spent memorizing the Quran, today's youth are more apt to be memorizing lyrics to the rock and roll music of the West. It is very evident to Islamic leaders that these outward behavioral changes reflect deep inward and spiritual adjustments impacting the lives of today's Muslim youth.

It should also be made clear that when Islamic leaders look at westerners, those who represent the source of this cultural onslaught, they generally see only the worst. As any regular viewer of the evening news back home can witness, what tends to be reported in the media is quite negative. Whereas those resident in America and other western nations balance the negative reports with the good they see for themselves on a daily basis, outsiders viewing the West from media sources alone tend to receive an overpoweringly negative message. For example, the many Roman Catholic priests who lead lives of quiet devotion while sacrificially serving their people do not make news, while the few who rape children entrusted to their care do. Similarly, the fact that many American students have fought for the right to lead or attend Bible studies on public school property goes unreported, while the few incidents involving school shootings make headlines for weeks.

The view that the undeniable momentum toward moral and spiritual decline among their own people can be directly attributed to cultural diffusion from the West, coupled with the view of westerners as reprehensible infidels, has been responsible for an intense hatred of western civilization on the part of many devout Muslims. This is especially true for Quranic Muslims who take adherence to spiritual purity very seriously. Many in such circles have come to the conclusion that coexistence with the West is impossible if conservative Islamic civilization is to flourish. Some have gone as far as to say that the continued dominance of western civilization will inevitably result in the complete eradication of true Islamic civilization.

At this point it is important to remember the very clear teaching within Islam that all true Muslims are responsible to defend the Ummah when and where it comes under attack. The position of militant Islam is that the Ummah has been under attack for centuries, and that the persecution has taken on extreme intensification over the last generation through the strategic spread of western culture. Those who adopt this view strongly believe that if Islamic civilization is to survive, no alternative exists aside from ensuring the complete destruction or comprehensive subjugation of western nations.

The troubling part for many westerners who begin to understand this argument concerns the realization that it makes so much sense. There really is no way to stem the tide of cultural diffusion aside from the impossible task of completely isolating vast populations. Even if such an alternative were feasible, it must be understood that moderate Islamic leaders, who generally hold power throughout the Islamic world, vehemently argue that advanced technology is necessary for development, and liberal Islamic groups teach that Islam can, indeed, thrive in a thoroughly modernized democratic world. In this way, militant Muslims find themselves facing enemies no matter where they turn.

Facing the realities outlined above in light of the very specific revelation concerning the duty of all true Muslims to defend Islam, it is completely understandable that many Quranic Muslims have chosen the path of militancy. To understand them, it is vital to see that in their minds there is no option if traditional Islam is to survive the clear and present threat represented by the spread of western values. The war being waged against western civilization by militant Muslims, then, should be understood as an effort by well-networked groups of devout people to ensure the continuance of their way of life rather than the insane actions of a few mentally unstable fanatics undertaking random acts of terrorism.

Chapter Eight

A Blueprint for Destruction

The manner in which western governments and media sources continue, even many months after the attack, to blame small groups of terrorists for the events of September 11, 2001, clearly demonstrates the brilliance of those ultimately responsible for what took place. The truth is that the events of that fateful morning and similar acts that will take place in the future are part of a well organized effort on the part of militant Muslims to achieve their goal of the destruction or subjugation of western nations in defense of Islam. To the extent that westerners ignore or misunderstand this reality, they play directly into the hands of their enemy. A key element of the elaborate plan to destroy the West rests on the assumption that western leaders lack the sophistication to understand that anything other than a well-defined nation-state or states with geographical borders can possibly represent a serious threat to their continued existence.

Finding Pieces

The first part of this work outlined how, during my fieldwork as a cultural anthropologist, I unintentionally gathered pieces to the puzzle that would eventually diagram what I call the blueprint for the destruction of western civilization. Having pieced together a good portion of the puzzle, I then began intentionally seeking the missing parts. As shared earlier, through an extraordinary set of circumstances I was given the missing pieces in 1996 by a man whom I had known for many years, and who it turns out had for some time participated in the development and realization of the blueprint itself.

Over the next few years, while resident in the developing world, I carefully watched the plans unfold exactly as they had been diagramed. So clear was the blueprint that I developed the ability to, at certain times, predict the next moves of those seeking to follow it. To my horror I found that what had been a fascinating intellectual exercise for several years had turned into a hobby by which I could explain events responsible for the lives of thousands of innocent people. Upon returning to the United States in the summer of 2001, I sought to communicate what I had learned with those I thought should know. Each effort, however, was met with either silence or disbelief. It was very clear that Americans had a very strong sense of invulnerability, and that any message concerning a threat to our way of life would continue to fall on deaf ears.

On the morning of September 11, 2001, a serious attitude adjustment took place. Since that time it seems everyone wants to know why the events happened and to be assured that such attacks could never happen again. I have sought in previous chapters to explain the reasons for the attacks. I will now demonstrate that they can best be understood as simply one stage of a very detailed set of plans.

Networks

At some point, most likely in the early 1980s, a group of well-placed leaders of militant Islam met to discuss a problem. As intellectuals and keen students of politics and history they understood very clearly that the future of traditional Islam was in jeopardy. It had become obvious to all that years of westernization and the spread of technology had been responsible for tremendous cultural changes in Islamic lands. It was equally clear that these changes were having a markedly negative impact on Quranic Islam, that thousands were abandoning traditions of faith for modern, sinful ways. It was recognized that to do nothing would mean that the momentum toward spiritual decay would continue and traditional Islam would eventually lose tremendous ground.

What had brought these men together was the shared view that westernization and the associated evils represented a clear and present danger to the Ummah. It had already been agreed that these processes demonstrably represented an attack on Islam, and that the Quranic imperative to defend the faith through warfare must be implemented.

Since western civilization was responsible for the attack, the answer was to destroy it as quickly as possible so that Islamic civilization could once again take its rightful place as the world's dominant cultural and intellectual force. The question concerned the steps that should be taken to realize this shared vision.

The first step concerned the establishment of a network of like-minded leaders representing Quranic Islam in various regions of the world. These men would be responsible for sharing the vision in their homelands and feeling out the individuals and groups that may be invited to participate. It is important for westerners to understand that such a network does not actually exist on paper. With the exception of the original group, which may well have only included a handful of men, the entire network, as I understand it, represents a loose and fluid web of relationships rather than an organization to which one would pledge membership. This is important to understand for two reasons. First, the concept of plausible deniability is a hallmark of the strategy by which these men operate. If no actual organization exists, the network cannot be held responsible for the actions of any individuals involved in what might later be characterized as "friendly talks." The other reason that a formal organization is undesirable concerns the manner in which decisions are reached. The network is by no means to be understood as representing a western style corporate model in which decisions are made at high levels and passed down to subordinates. Rather, the model adopted more resembles the Islamic ideal of reaching decisions by consensus as was common in the tribal councils of Muhammad's day and in the formal

Islamic organizations of today. The benefit of such a model is that groups casually associated with the informal network can receive subtle direction from the more intellectual members, and yet plan specifics on their own. This "relationship" allows for a strong sense of ownership for any actions taken, despite the reality that the timing and targets may well have been tactically planned by the more highly-placed participants in the network.

The practical outworking of this may be seen in the case of Osama bin Laden and his al-Qaeda "network." For the sake of argument we might assume that bin Laden himself knows very little about the original group of militant intellectuals who sit atop a loose, global network of like-minded groups spanning the globe. Having caught the original vision, bin Laden sets up a more structured group of militants over which he and a few others enjoy a degree of direct leadership. During leadership councils attended by one or two visiting like-minded men of some international stature, bin Laden and his council might receive suggestions concerning the view that using jumbo jets to destroy buildings would be a great way to use the infidels' own technology against them. At other meetings attended by yet other "friends," when the idea of using airplanes against the West is brought up by bin Laden, specific targets might be suggested by the visitors as having excellent symbolic value in such an attack. Finally, at yet other informal meetings issues of timing might be offered based on factors having to do with economic and political issues. The question of whether or not bin Laden himself realizes the full extent of the larger network is of little importance.

The fact that he and his leaders could take ownership of the September 11th attacks is justifiable, despite the reality that the initial planning may have happened at a much more intellectual and highly-placed level. The core of this global network of militant Islam, then, should be understood more as a "think-tank" with direction-setting goals than as a level of structured leadership that can be identified or held responsible for specific acts aimed at western targets.

Having taken the initial step of establishing an ever expanding and at times contracting network of militant groups across the globe, the next issue facing the original group concerned the adoption of a specific, long-term strategy to destroy western powers.

It is believed by many that if Muslims and infidels met on the field of battle on equal terms that Muslims would win every time. This is due principally to the view that Allah has promised success for those who fight in the cause of Islam, but also to the belief that Muslim warriors are inherently superior to those fighting for lesser causes. The realization that meeting the West on equal terms represents a serious problem is obvious to all involved. It is well understood that the West has superior numbers when compared to those who can be counted on to actually take the field in direct military action against them. It is also recognized that history has, however unjustly, favored the West in terms of technological advancement. With this in mind the two issues involved in ensuring equal terms, and the resulting victory, involve technology and numbers.

Technology

The fact that western nations possess a tremendous technological advantage over Islamic nations is undeniable. This imbalance was even more noticeable in the early 1980s than it is today. The question facing those hoping to destroy the West concerned how the playing field could be leveled. The answer hints at the brilliance and patience of those involved.

It is realized that the West did not achieve technological sophistication overnight, but that it took many generations to develop the advantage now enjoyed. Despite this reality, it is understood that the advances gained to date must be passed on to each succeeding generation of young, western minds. The institutions primarily responsible for this transfer of knowledge from one generation to the next are western universities. With this in mind, it seemed an elegant solution to the original group of thinkers that a certain percentage of the best and brightest students from within the ranks of Quranic and militant Islam should be sent to the West to acquire the technological knowledge being passed on to westerners.

Following this strategy, those involved hand picked young men and women from various areas to attend western universities and specialize in certain fields of learning. As I understand it, many were chosen to study almost every field listed in university catalogs. In this way every discipline from accounting to zoology would be covered by many Muslim students. The fact that fields such as economics, political science, civil engineering, and nuclear physics fall within the a to z list was not lost on these men.

The decision to send many students for each field can be

attributed to the realization that some would become enamored with the West and never return, and that others might not be open in later life to the militant vision. It is important when discussing these issues to make very clear that when considering the number of hand-picked individuals involved in this strategy, they represent a very small percentage of Islamic students studying in the West. This discussion should in no way lead anyone to believe that the thousands of hard-working Muslim students who study today in the West are in any way involved in such strategies. The other factor to remember is that the students themselves were almost certainly not aware of why they had been chosen. They were a small percentage of the millions of other young people who desired to be educated in the West. For reasons of security, it would make perfect sense that such students would be unaware of the hope that they would one day contribute to the militant vision.

Over the ensuing decades, the network of militancy grew as problems between western nations and Islamic peoples continued to arise. This being the case, a small percentage of those educated in the West eventually found themselves joining the ranks of militant Islam and using their training to fulfill what they consider to be the will of Allah.

Numbers

Together with the original thinkers, the few western-trained militant specialists set to work on the next issue that stood in the way of a level playing field. Militant groups still accounted for a very small percentage of Islam. The question of how to get Quranic Muslims involved in the fight concerned the reality that they did not perceive Islam as being under direct attack from the West. If this perception could be replaced by outrage on the part of Quranic Muslims as a result of direct military action by the West against Islam, it was understood that the ranks of militant Islam would swell, eventually including Quaranic and cultural Muslims alike. The strategy, then, involves creating situations in which western governments are enticed into taking direct, forceful military action against Muslim populations. The elegance of the resulting blueprint can only be appreciated when understood as being developed by militant Muslims as a means by which western powers would ultimately be responsible for their own destruction.

The initial stages of the plan involved undertaking selective acts of terrorism against key targets in the developing world. The contributions of those trained in the West to these efforts cannot be overemphasized. When conditions were judged to be perfect based on various criteria, the acts would be implemented according to the suggestions of specialists in fields such as economics, political science, and the social sciences. Those trained in technical specialties would lend their expertise to questions of how damage could be optimized to ensure the desired results.

The acts were to be undertaken in such a manner as to ensure that everyone understood that Muslims were to blame, but that no specific group could be identified. In this way, the inevitable retaliation would be aimed at Muslims in general and would be seen as arbitrary acts without justification. Perceiving these retaliatory strikes as unjustified actions against innocent members of the Ummah, Muslims from both Quranic and cultural circles would recognize their responsibility to defend their fellow Muslims in particular and Islam in general. The hope is that such situations would spread, that armed conflict between Muslims and infidels would result, and that Muslims from other areas would join the fight, thus ensuring level playing fields in limited areas.

The net result of such actions would be ground gained for Muslims and the realization on the part of the faithful that Allah will come to their aid if they simply choose to fight in His cause. Having set such circumstances in motion in one area, the next step involved studying the entire situation for weak points before moving on to repeat the process in yet another part of the developing world. As time went on and such actions were taken within developing nations, the manner in which plausible deniability, optimum retaliation, mass participation on the part of outraged Muslims, and concrete political and geographic gains through resulting armed conflict could be ensured were constantly studied for enhancement.

September 11th in Context

Lessons learned in the developing world would be directly applied to the next stage of the blueprint: taking the now perfected process to the West. After a few false starts involving various airplane bombings and the failed attempt to destroy the World Trade Center in February 1993, the attacks of September 11, 2001, should be understood as fitting perfectly into the blueprint outlined above.

The goal of enticing the United States into taking direct military action against Islamic nations could best be realized if strikes against the country were very damaging and aimed at targets representing institutions of immense symbolic importance to the American people. Anything less would cause liberal congressional leaders to argue that retaliatory strikes must be limited in their scope, thus lessoning the outrage of Muslims and their resulting desire to join in the fight against western infidels.

The involvement of various specialists in the timing is also apparent. Economically the United States was, in September 2001, on the brink of recession. Politically, the nation had a new president whose very legitimacy to rule had been questioned by a significant percentage of Americans. Militarily, the nation was judged to have been at its weakest state since World War II. This combination of factors would lead to the conclusion that September 2001 represented the perfect time to strike a tremendous blow to the United States of America.

In addition to issues of timing, the targets chosen reveal a tremendous amount of strategic planning. Muslim economists understand well that the United States economy is closely tied with the stock market, and that Wall Street rises and falls to a significant degree on the whims of individual investors who ride the waves of political and economic stability. The destruction of the symbolic heart of the American economy and the epicenter of the United States military leadership, together with what was certain to be a failure of leadership on the part of an untested president would almost certainly result, so it was thought, in the total collapse of the American economy. Had the target of the White House or Capital building been hit as well, the crisis of leadership, crash of the economy, and resulting loss of millions of jobs would stand an even greater chance of having been realized. In such a scenario, retaliatory strikes would almost certainly be massive and appallingly brutal to satiate the appetite of an outraged American public, thus playing right into the hands of those who developed the blueprint for destruction.

The way that President Bush valiantly rose to the occasion and proved himself to be every inch a great leader was almost certainly a surprise to those who planned the attacks. In a similar way, who could have imagined that the devastating loss of life and destruction experienced in New York City would be met by a strong message of hope offered by Mayor Giuliani. The courageous leadership of these men, coupled with the heroic actions of brave emergency response personnel and the resulting sense of unity on the part of the American people, worked against the plans of bin Laden and his organization. In addition, it should be understood that the Taliban regime was very unpopular within much of the Islamic world. The way that some degree of responsibility for the attacks was attributed to them, and that they, therefore, served as a scapegoat with regard to retaliatory strikes, also worked against the plans outlined in the blueprint.

The ingenious nature of the blueprint can be seen, however, in the fact that it does not have to work the first, second, or even fiftieth time. Be assured that those at the planning levels of the network of international militant

Islam are working diligently to ensure that every possible lesson is learned from the "failures" associated with September 11, 2001, and that the next strike will be aimed at ensuring a more "successful" result.

For example, were I to guess at what is now being planned by the leaders of militant Islam, I would expect that President Bush himself will be targeted as part of yet another comprehensive attack. This is thought to be necessary because it was President Bush's leadership that, to a large extent, accounted for the remarkable manner in which Americans dealt with the tragedy. In future attacks the death of a president would help insure, so it might be thought, that a more chaotic situation would result than would otherwise be the case. Washington, DC, would most likely be targeted as well since it represents the location most associated with "failure" in the initial attack. Just as the World Trade Center's 1993 failure was "rectified" in 2001, I would expect ensuing attacks to focus on the areas "missed" on September 11th.

Thinking through the events with the blueprint in mind, I often wonder if the US Capital building may have been considered as a possible target for the September 11th attacks. Imagine the impact on our government if a high percentage of United States senators and representatives had been killed on that morning. The tremendous task of having to install new congressional leaders at a moments notice would almost certainly have resulted in a far more chaotic situation than that experienced. With this in mind I would expect the Capital building to be considered a high-priority target in future attacks, along with President Bush and a host of other highly symbolic targets aimed at causing outrage and panic on the part of the American public.

A related issue concerns the fact that many Muslim strategists believe that Americans will accept almost anything that does not directly and negatively impact their financial situation. For this reason, I would expect future attacks to be aimed at triggering the massive job losses that would almost certainly have resulted from the crash of the stock market had the initial attack gone more according to plan. According to the blueprint, a scenario in which millions of Americans wake to find their president and many congressional leaders fallen, the stock market in ruins, and their individual jobs no longer available would result in the massive retaliatory strikes against Islamic nations that might well bring enough Muslims into the fight to ensure a more level playing field.

It bears pointing out yet again that a key strength of the blueprint is that it can be repeated until it brings about the desired result. Just as on December 6, 1941, most Americans felt the war in Europe was an event in which they did not wish to be involved, so most Muslims today do not see the need to join the militant struggle against western powers. What militant strategists hope and plan for is a Pearl Harbor-like event that will motivate their fellow believers the way that December 7th, 1941 caused most Americans to agree that massive involvement in World War II was suddenly essential.

The chances that any major undertaking will succeed depends to a large degree on the character of those attempting to realize the stated objectives. I can recall, for example, many times when various friends have shared plans to establish a new business or build a certain dream home, yet the plans never seemed to materialize. There are others I have known, however, who after sharing such plans actually took steps to reach their goals. Those who represent the latter group tend to have a character trait not common among those in the former. The trait I refer to is that of confidence. When I consider the men I have known in either Quaranic or militant circles of influence, I can say without hesitation that confidence is by no means in short supply. To the contrary, these men, certain of the righteous nature of their calling or cause, are supremely confident that they have the blessings of Allah as they endeavor to do His will. As I think back on the conversation I had with Hasan in which he so carefully provided the details I had been missing, I recall both his confident demeanor and the awe, perhaps even fear, apparent in his eyes as he assured me that the plans would ultimately succeed. The reality that a well-thought-out blueprint rests in the hands of such confident men is enough to convince me that they will do all within their power to see it through to the end or willingly die in the effort.

Chapter Nine

Distinct Advantages

One of the privileges offered to those who make the study of history a priority is the ability to learn vicariously. This is especially true with regard to military history. As one makes a study of the great victories and failures of the past with the purpose of applying knowledge gained to the present, lessons learned can have a tremendous impact on helping to ensure triumphant results in future struggles.

Understanding the Enemy

It has been suggested that one of the lessons Americans learned the hard way through the Vietnam War is the absolute necessity to understand one's enemy and the principles on which his strategies are based. Among this and other insights gained in that conflict, I believe those who fought so valiantly there would argue that "all the king's horses and all the king's men" will by no means ensure victory if such troops are trained and equipped to fight according to the doctrines of conventional warfare when the enemy refuses to meet them on these terms. The losses experienced by American troops thrown into a conflict that few were trained to fight should serve to remind us of the importance of understanding our enemy and his tactics before attempting to engage him in any large-scale conflict. This is particularly important to understand in a day and age in which America's military superiority and "superpower" status remains relatively unchallenged. The thought that United States troops can easily handle any situation that may arise by means of technological superiority and sheer strength alone represents a dangerous underestimation of the realities that exist outside our borders.

Just as the original group of militant Muslims who targeted the West understood that their enemies held certain advantages, so it is vital for westerners today to realize that those following the blueprint outlined in the previous chapter also enjoy a number of very real advantages. To ignore this reality is to invite losses that might otherwise have been avoidable.

War by Any Other Name

The first advantage enjoyed by the militant Muslims who have targeted the West concerns the nature of the strategy they have chosen to adopt. For lack of a better phrase I will refer to this approach as "Strategic Provocation and Retaliation" warfare, or SPAR for short.

Unlike the use of harassment and ambush by small, armed groups against occupying forces as is common in Guerilla warfare for the purpose of inflicting damage or disrupting supply lines, SPAR warfare is based on very different tactics aimed at very different ends. The core doctrine of SPAR warfare is based on the use of terrorist attacks against highly symbolic targets located in an enemy's home territory in order to provoke massive retaliation with the ultimate goal of ensuring conventional warfare on more equal terms. The approach assumes the existence of vast potential, yet unmotivated, troops available to the perpetrators and is directly aimed at motivating such troops to join the conflict by means of ensuring that retaliatory strikes are directed toward them.

I suppose an example would be a situation in which a member of the Hatfield clan desired to start a feud with the McCoy clan, yet could not talk his "kinfolk" into believing that such an effort would be worthwhile. Having taunted the McCoys on their home turf, and then firing a shot through their kitchen window, the Hatfield boy would then flee home, sure that a large group of McCoys would be in hot pursuit ready to trash the Hatfield homestead, and thus beginning the feud. The ingenuity evident in this strategy involves the fact that the McCoys may never realize that the instigator acted alone, and that he does not represent the true desires of the Hatfield clan. In the same way, the Hatfield clan is unaware that it was one of their own that fired the first shot for the purposes of beginning a feud. All they know is the obvious fact that the McCoys are attacking their homestead. This oversimplified fictional scenario serves to demonstrate the reality that to the degree the McCoy family does not understand what is actually taking place, the lone Hatfield boy has a very real advantage over the entire McCoy clan. It should also be noted that once the feud has begun, every act undertaken by either side can be rightly justified as an act of self defense.

When one views the events involved in the Palestinian-Israeli conflict as a prime example of SPAR warfare aimed at enlisting the assistance of larger Islamic nations against Israel, the suicide bombings and other "terrorist" acts begin to make strategic sense. As Israeli retaliations grow increasingly brutal aimed at once and for all ending acts of terrorism, the cry of the Palestinians that they are being systematically slaughtered begins to motivate other nations toward action against Israel. Understanding that Israel has no choice but to retaliate in no way lessens the outrage of those who see such actions as unjustifiable, and the "martyr missions" as acts of defiance against a stronger, infidel opponent. The situation for Israel is an impossible one to win. As long as there are individuals willing to trade their own life for the cause, retaliations will continue, and the day when warfare at a much higher level begins will draw ever closer.

Using the same strategy against the United States and Europe, one can imagine a scenario in which ever increasing terrorist attacks result in ever more brutal and comprehensive retaliatory strikes, thus resulting in warfare on a much larger scale. In the absence of a comprehensive understanding of, and response to, SPAR warfare, western powers will undoubtedly play directly into the hands of those who have created this strategy to bring about the desired results.

Phantom Powers

A second advantage enjoyed by the global network of militant Islam is that since no formal umbrella organization exists, assigning responsibility for future attacks will grow increasingly more difficult as those who undertake them learn from past mistakes.

A good deal of the "failure" associated with the September 11th attacks from the viewpoint of militant Islam has to do with the way that retaliatory strikes were understood by the international community, including almost all Islamic nations, as justifiable. Imagine how differently Islamic nations would have responded if retaliatory strikes had been aimed at Saudi Arabia since a good number of the hijackers were Saudi nationals. As the caretaker nation of Islam's most holy sites, an attack on Saudi Arabia would almost certainly have been viewed as an attack on Islam itself, thus causing many Islamic nations to consider all manner of desperate measures against the United States. It is certain that just as the technical failures of the first World Trade Center bombing were addressed and rectified, so these more recent problems will be studied and resolved as well. One would fully expect that future attacks would be far more difficult to pin on certain groups, thus making any retaliation appear all the more arbitrary and outrageous.

Of related interest is the fact that there is no reason to think that future attacks may not include very real evidence leading to false conclusions. For example, it is not outside the realm of possibility to imagine a scenario in which a militant group from elsewhere in Asia is able to illegally obtain materials for a small-scale nuclear weapon in Pakistan. Assembling and detonating the weapon on their own as part of a massive SPAR attack, every effort might be made to ensure that the bomb can be traced directly back to Pakistan, thus ensuring that retaliation be targeted on a nation whose only crime may have been inefficient security and accounting measures.

With this and a thousand other similar scenarios in mind, it is simple to understand how the almost impossible task of assigning ultimate responsibility for specific acts represents a very real advantage for militant Islam.

A New Domino Theory

As if SPAR warfare itself and the covert nature of those ultimately responsible for attacks were not enough of an advantage, it should be understood that militant Islamic groups enjoy yet another factor that very much favors their efforts over those of the West. This factor is that the near-term objective of these groups is simply the destruction of western civilization.

No matter how unfair it may seem, the laws of physics undeniably demonstrate the reality that it is far easier to destroy something than it is to either build or protect it. Take, for example, a room full of dominos set on their edges in close proximity to one another. It may well take weeks of back-breaking labor to set up a complex arrangement of dominos capable of thrilling an audience when it is finally set in motion and all the pieces fall on top of one another. Despite the many hours spent in preparation, the destruction of the elaborate arrangement can be initiated by the simple flick of a finger striking a single, strategically placed domino.

The same law of physics holds true for what we might call the Twin-Tower Principle. Anyone who ever visited New York City's Twin Towers prior to September 11th, 2001, will understand the opinion that they stood as a prime example of architectural genius. Soaring into the sky, the buildings represented perhaps as many as one hundred million man-hours when all the stages of construction are taken into account. Despite the enormous efforts the buildings represented, it took only forty minutes or so for them to be destroyed when hit in just the right manner.

When one thinks of western civilization as the culmination of thousands of years of development, it is tempting to hold the view that something that took so long to establish would certainly take hundreds of years to destroy. However difficult it is to ponder such thoughts, the truth is that western civilization is no less fragile, nor its continuance any more guaranteed, than the countless other civilizations that have long since faded into history.

The Sanity Factor

For many years now I have had the privilege of being able to count several law enforcement officers as close friends. I very much enjoy conversations with these unbelievably brave men in which they recount the exploits of various criminals and the manner in which they were eventually captured. One thing that always fascinates me is that so many criminals are caught due to blind stupidity. I recall one account of how through intense planning and meticulous implementation a man was able to successfully rob a bank of many thousands of dollars. Having made good his escape, the man may well have been thinking as he drove down an interstate whether he should first purchase a luxury car or an expensive boat with the money he so skillfully earned. Apparently pondering such issues a bit too deeply, or perhaps in a subconscious effort to work off the adrenaline that must have been coursing through his veins, the bandit found himself driving at a very high rate of speed despite the fact that he was by now well removed from the scene of his crime. It so happens that just a few minutes before, a highway patrolman had set up his radar gun looking for speeders. As the bandit's car sped past the trooper's patrol vehicle, the gun registered the speed, and what might have been a routine stop eventually ended with the apprehension of a dangerous felon. Having demonstrated his genius for planning just hours before, the man was captured for what must appear to him now as a very foolish mistake.

A somewhat similar principle seems to operate in criminals of a different nature. I remember listening to an interview with an agent of the Federal Bureau of Investigation who aided in the apprehension of several serial killers. As I listened carefully to the accounts of how the murderers were captured, the common theme had to do with the fact that each had suffered in some way from deep psychological problems. In every case, the criminal made some foolish error directly attributable to his mental condition, and this mistake is what eventually led to his capture. In other words, were these men sane individuals killing for political reasons rather than to satiate some deprived longing, they might still be free.

A case that perfectly illustrates this point is that of the Unabomber. An anarchist who hated science, industry and technology, Theodore Kaczynski killed three people and successfully terrorized many within the United States for well over sixteen years. Placing the question of his mental health aside for a moment, it is instructive to note that this former Harvard student and university mathematics professor was apparently motivated primarily by ideological reasons rather than the more perverted stimuli common to most serial killers. This may account for the reason that it was only after Kaczynski decided to stop killing and publish his lengthy manifesto that law enforcement agents, after spending more than fifty million dollars, were able to identify and apprehend him.

Applying these lessons to a fictional scenario, imagine for a moment there existed a highly intelligent university professor whose mental health is perfectly ordinary. Further imagine that this man's family, while on vacation in a major city, had been killed through a bizarre set of circumstances surrounding the arrest of a drug dealer. Approaching the normal retirement age and financially set for life, the man eventually leaves his university position and decides to devote the remainder of his life to assassinating drug dealers. Seeing his new calling as an intellectual challenge, the professor meticulously plans every detail of each "hit" to ensure that no evidence exists linking him to the "crimes." One might imagine that in such a situation our fictional vigilante-professor may well continue executing his form of justice until advanced age makes it no longer possible.

The point of mentioning these macabre situations and scenarios involves the fact that a common misconception concerning the "terrorists" responsible for the events of September 11, 2001, is that they are mentally unstable individuals. The importance of understanding that this is not the case concerns the reality that it would be far easier to stop them if it were true. To the contrary, I would argue that the men responsible for developing and implementing the blueprint for destruction more closely fit the profile of our fictional professor than they do the profiles common to most serial killers. I can testify that most of the men I have personally known within the realm of militant Islam are very clear thinkers indeed. This is especially true of those in top leadership positions. Whether trained in theology, law, the social sciences, or fields of a more technical nature, these men generally have the ability to apply pragmatic solutions to highly complex situations.

A Very Real Virtue

In addition to the advantages outlined above, perhaps the factor that most favors militant Muslims concerns something that is so uncommon in the western world. I refer here to the issue of patience.

If there ever existed a society in which people desired to achieve goals or acquire goods more quickly than is common to those of us in the United States, I am unaware of it. Whether it concerns fast food, quick profits, or immediate retaliation, it seems Americans are in a desperate hurry to get satisfaction. I am by no means suggesting that this character trait that has become such a normative part of our culture is always negative. How else could Americans have led the world in the developments that account for the progression from horse carts to the space shuttle in less than a century?

The passion for progress and forward motion that seems so common to Americans can, however, have negative consequences in certain situations. By way of evidence I cite the reaction on the part of civil authorities to the events of September 11, 2001. In the immediate aftermath of the destruction, it seems that everything having to do with security changed overnight. Whether it concerned guarding large sources of drinking water or the elimination of the ever popular "Skycap" option for checking luggage into airports, major changes were implemented immediately. Within ten days, however, many of the nation's sources of drinking water were once again unguarded, and Skycaps were again a normal part of operations at many airports. The question is, what took place on day nine that ensured that threats to such things no longer existed? The issue seems to be that those in authority decided that the immediate threat of further terrorist attacks had ended.

This short attention span on the part of Americans is very much recognized and appreciated by those who count themselves our enemies. It should be remembered that Americans are facing an enemy who still vividly recalls events of the Crusades that took place many centuries ago, and who initiated a blueprint that by design could not be put into effect for many years.

To the degree that Americans and others hope to gain a deeper understanding of those known as our "new enemies," it is vital to realize that these groups enjoy several key advantages as they undertake their efforts. To underestimate the capabilities of militant groups represents a very serious error in judgment that may well have grave, long-term consequences if not recognized and corrected.

Chapter Ten

Inherent Limitations

Much of the information presented in the preceding chapters represents a sober look at the realities facing the West as leaders and citizens come to terms with the true nature of those who have targeted them for destruction. There is no question that militant Muslims are numerous, are led by brilliant men who have spent many years developing well-organized plans to accomplish their goals, and that they enjoy several key advantages as they undertake their efforts. It is also true, however, that the strategies now at work against the West include several key limitations. Recognizing the weak points inherent in the strategy adopted by militant Muslims may offer insights into how the West might best respond as the plans continue to unfold.

Working the Borders

The point has been made that the dividing lines separating

cultural, Quranic, and militant Islam are not hard and clear. To the contrary, they should be more accurately understood as porous borders subject to "leakage" as events unfold that push those within them in one direction or another. The following diagram may serve to illustrate this point:

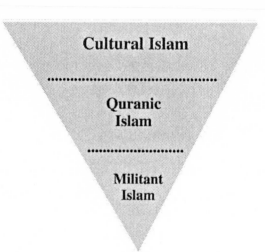

The goal for militant Muslims as they engage in what I call Strategic Provocation and Retaliation warfare is to push as many Quranic and cultural Muslims as possible "south" toward militancy. The thinking is that as the borders shift and millions join the cause, more conventional-style armed conflict on more equal terms will be made possible.

A key limitation intrinsic to this strategy concerns the fact that the border between Quranic and militant Islam is "manned" by leaders more prone to engage in theological debate than hand-to-hand combat. The job of motivating "men of letters" to drop their first love and join men of action in destructive exploits represents a significant challenge. The strategic importance of succeeding in this task concerns the reality that many of these men have tremendous followings. Winning them over, therefore, is equivalent to recruiting millions of highly motivated and disciplined men very willing to give their lives should their leaders endorse the cause.

I have spent countless hours in the company of the men sitting on this all-important border. It was they who represented the focus of most of my years of fieldwork in Islamic lands. I have watched such men grapple with the weighty issues involving how they will respond to the militant call. The task of "winning over" these leaders to militancy is by no means an easy one. I believe most of them simply want to be left alone to teach Islam as they sense they have been called to do.

Understanding the nature and inclinations of these learned men, it makes sense to take their views into account when considering how best to respond to the threat of militant Islam. A key part of any successful strategy aimed at limiting the impact of militant Islam will involve efforts toward turning these leaders against those who have targeted western civilization for destruction. A major problem is that the West has, for many decades, worked very diligently to ensure just the opposite.

Looking at the world through the perspective of Muslim leaders, it is clear that western powers are responsible for many of the challenges facing Muslim populations. This is not only true for cultural issues fueling the moral decline of Muslim youth, but also for economic factors impacting the lives of their parents.

I remember as a child reading of the thousands of West Virginia farmers who in the late 19th century left their lands for an opportunity to work for large coal mining corporations. After working for many years and attempting to feed and clothe their growing families, many such men eventually found themselves working long hours to little or no advantage. Through the combination of low wages and high prices, many of them were perpetually in debt to the company store. In the same way, many thousands of men, women, and at times children, in Islamic and other lands are today trapped in a similar no-win situation as they continually work fourteen-hour days in factories owned by western corporations. Earning the equivalent of just a few dollars each day, many Muslims struggle through life so that Americans can have the privilege of being seen in the latest style of athletic footwear costing well over one hundred dollars a pair. Regardless of any political-economic circumstances that might ultimately be responsible for such situations, the reality that Americans wear the products manufactured by Muslims working under abysmal conditions is enough of a reason to point the finger of blame westward. In order to better understand the outrage associated with situations like this, imagine if many thousands of American men, women and children found themselves working fourteen-hour days six days each week in an endless cycle so that Muslim women in Saudi Arabia could wear the latest fashion in head-coverings. In such a situation, it is not difficult to imagine that less than sympathetic views concerning these consumers would be popular.

Making their living under conditions like those outlined

above, working diligently to limit the impact of western cultural practices and values observed by their children through various forms of entertainment, and hearing of seemingly unjustified military strikes undertaken by western powers against other Muslims, it is not difficult to understand how seeds of militancy can take root among many Islamic populations.

The fact is that through what is perceived to be the economic exploitation of Muslims in developing nations, the increasingly observable moral degeneration and spread of western culture, and our lack of knowledge concerning what enrages Muslims most, westerners have for years been working very hard to push Quranic leaders into the category of militant Islam. In this way westerners are actually working against what might be seen as a major weakness in the strategies adopted by those who count themselves our enemies.

With these facts in mind, even the simplest efforts taken to address issues such as those listed above would go a long way toward building bridges of understanding between people of the West and leaders of Quranic Islam. An example might include the very visible establishment and funding of educational facilities for those working in and around western-owned manufacturing facilities in the developing world. When speaking with young Muslims who have grown very disillusioned with the West, one often hears stories of how they sought opportunities to study in Europe or America. Many who seek such opportunities are angrily turned away by representatives of foreign governments. The distinct impression is often received that the officials consider the students unworthy of such a high honor. Offering these students an opportunity to study in their own lands under western teachers would go a long way toward establishing mutual respect.

In addition, efforts to clearly justify military actions against targets in Islamic nations should continue to be a high priority. In this regard, an excellent job was done by the Bush administration in the wake of the September 11th attacks. Great efforts were made by American leaders to make clear that retaliatory actions were aimed at those directly responsible for the attacks and not against the religion of Islam or Muslim peoples in general. Despite the success of these efforts, however, as this book is being written it seems apparent that plans are underway to ride the wave of "anti-terrorist" sentiment as American military strategists argue that this may be a good time to settle an old score in Iraq against Saddam Hussein. Such plans, if actually undertaken, may well be counterproductive to the larger issues involving the wisdom of taking into account how actions taken by western military powers are perceived by leaders of Quaranic Islam.

Numbers Equal Risk

In addition to the issues associated with having to motivate large numbers of people to join their cause, another problem for militant Muslims implementing the blueprint for destruction concerns the fact that as the number of those involved in the fight continues to grow, the number of familiar faces on the front lines begins to fall.

Up to this point in their struggle, those involved in militant

Islam have, to a large degree, been closely associated with one another for many years. In as much as a major part of their strategy involves tremendous numbers of new recruits, it is clear that to the extent they succeed, leaders within militant circles will be less sure of who it is they can trust with sensitive information. This is an especially important point during the stage at which more comprehensive attacks are planned. As more individuals are involved in such attacks, more people have to know what is being planned and where it will take place. It would take an extraordinarily sophisticated organizational effort to ensure complete secrecy. As was explained earlier, the very nature of associations within circles of militant Islam requires that formal organizational structures not exist. This inherent weakness can be exploited only if efforts are made right away to place intelligence assets at strategic points within the world of militant Islam. Since such efforts by their very nature take many years to accomplish, it would be a good decision on the part of western intelligence agencies to give top priority to these concerns if they have not already done so.

While one would hope that intelligence assets have been working within militant groups for many years, I can only say that my personal experience leads me to believe that we are well behind where we should be on these important issues. I say this due to the fact that my attempts over the years to share pertinent information have been met with cold disinterest on the part of those who should be most interested. I have heard similar reports from others who have had the opportunity to gain insights and information through many years of close relationships within the Islamic world. As much as we would love to think it accurate, it seems just possible that the stereo-typical Hollywood view of intelligence communities staffed with handsome spies who dash off to the latest global hotspot in order to single-handedly save the world has been subject to at least some degree of exaggeration. Although I cannot speak with authority to issues involving other communities of the world, I can say that making significant inroads into the ranks of militant Islam will require substantial, long-term efforts on the part of very patient and determined individuals willing to take enormous risks.

A Distorted View

The remaining limitation inherent to the strategy under-taken by militant Muslims in their efforts to destroy western civilization concerns their opinions of westerners in general and Americans in particular.

The point has been made elsewhere in this work that to a surprising degree what Muslims know of America has been learned through media sources. These include magazines, newspapers, news broadcasts, television shows, and even Hollywood movies. As absurd as it may seem, the reality that such sources present a less than realistic view of what life is actually like in the United States seems to have been lost on many within the Islamic world. Whether for this or any number of other reasons, the salient point is that many militant Muslims have a very distorted view concerning the core values shared by most Americans. The realm in which this view becomes important to our discussion has to do with issues of vigilance and the will of American soldiers to fight. The assumption is that, owing to the influence of liberal politicians and the lack of a serious threat, America's military preparedness is at its lowest level since World War II and that the troops themselves will be unwilling to fight when they are actually ordered to do so.

With the exception of the small number of well-trained American special forces units, I believe it would be accurate to say that many Muslims see American soldiers as inherently inferior to the average Muslim warrior fighting for the cause of Allah. The few situations in recent history, such as the Persian Gulf War, in which American forces fought directly against Muslim soldiers are seen as pitiful examples of Muslims serving the belligerent causes of a renegade leader as opposed to men of principle serving Almighty God. Understanding that the playing field was by no means level in that particular conflict also fits into the argument that it in no way represents what may be expected in future encounters.

In the same way that Americans have seriously underestimated the "new enemy" in the "War on Terror," I believe that leaders of militant Islam would be shocked to discover the truth concerning the depth and sophistication of resources available to the United States armed forces, despite the fact that the nation's overall state of military preparedness might not be all that many would consider ideal. In the same way, I am certain that when militant Muslims face American soldiers on future battlefields, even on equal terms, they will discover that the same spirit of faith and freedom responsible for establishing this great nation continues to beat strong in the hearts of America's fighting men and women.

The limitations noted above represent noteworthy chinks in what is otherwise a very well-built suit of armor. To the degree that such weaknesses can be exploited, a formidable enemy can be significantly weakened. To the degree they are overlooked by leaders who choose to ignore the very real threat of militant Islam, those who have chosen to destroy western civilization have a far greater chance of one day realizing their vision.

Chapter Eleven

Meeting the Challenge

The threat represented by militant Islam represents a challenge to the entire western world. It seems very clear that if it is to be successfully overcome, a new level of international cooperation will be necessary. Together with many nations, the United States and its traditional allies may be tested in a way that has not been known since the two previous world wars. The necessity for an international response to the challenges now facing the world notwithstanding, it is the United States that seems to have been singled out by militant Muslims as the nation most deserving of their attention.

There is no question that the events of September 11, 2001, represent a uniquely American tragedy. The thousands of lives lost, immense damage inflicted, and emotional scars now resident within the hearts of millions will be remembered for as long as American history is recorded.

To the extent that militant Muslims continue the implementation of their well-planned strategies, more of the same may
be expected. As Americans come to terms with this new
reality, an important question to consider is whether or not
any good can come from such adversity.

The Sleeping Giant

The 20th century was an important period of transition for
the United States in many significant ways. Having survived
the Civil War just over a generation earlier, Americans faced
the dawn of a new century with enthusiasm and ingenuity.
New inventions together with the continued development of
emerging technologies made possible an unprecedented
period of advancement. The tremendous challenges brought
about by World War I, a severe economic depression, and
World War II were met and overcome by generations of
American heroes. Even the prolonged and costly struggle
against Communism in what has become known as the Cold
War could not defeat the nation that emerged as the world's
only superpower. Since the destruction of the Berlin Wall in
1989, however, some would suggest that, lacking a significant challenge to its superpower status, America began to
relax after almost a century of intense forward progress. In
other words, it is as if after winning a beachhead through
heroic sacrifice and experiencing many casualties, American
soldiers were slowly replaced by vacationing crowds, and for
the past several years many have taken the opportunity to
enjoy a long nap on the warm sand. What is just now becoming evident is that while America rested, others were busy

training to take their place of world leadership. In this regard, the September 11th attacks can be understood as an attempt to kick sand in the face of a sleeping giant. Without doubt the aggressive move served to rouse America from its slumber, yet the question of how the nation will respond remains to be answered. After waking to swat a few bothersome flies will America roll over to resume its pleasant dream, or will it truly awaken to the realization that a significant challenger has arisen and has set his sights on taking the beach? To the degree that America can be stirred to action, to the extent that its citizens meet the challenges confronting them by redis-covering the faith and values of their founding fathers, there is hope that America's greatest days may lie in the future, rather than in ages past.

A New America

One of the great privileges of serving as an instructor in other nations is the opportunity to teach American history to non-American students. Sharing the thrilling story of how men and women who had everything to lose and only uncer-tainty to gain by declaring, fighting for, and eventually win-ning independence from one of the great world powers has a way of reminding one of just how special it is to be an American. The rich heritage shared by those who call the United States the land of their fathers is all the more cher-ished and appreciated when one resides in a far-off land and often finds himself longing for the nation of his birth. Those who have shared in such an experience sometimes find themselves lamenting the fact that more Americans cannot enjoy the thrill of living in a foreign culture for several years, and then returning home with a whole new appreciation for the blessings the United States has to offer. In the same way that those who do so quickly begin to once again take for granted the unique nature of our society, it seems that the average American who never leaves does not fully understand or appreciate that the life he or she lives represents something very unusual.

Life in America might best be described by a term one often hears, yet seldom stops to contemplate: freedom. One wonders whether or not Americans understand how uncommon it is to have the opportunity as an individual citizen to chart one's own path to the future. The fact that through hard work and determination most Americans can choose where to live and have access to a very comfortable lifestyle represents a rare privilege made possible by the sacrifices of previous generations. Just as Americans in those less settled days had far fewer personal choices, so today throughout the world a surprising number of people find themselves with very few individual alternatives. The thought that one can simply choose to succeed is unimaginable for much of the world's population. The reality that freedom was, for the most part, won for Americans by the sacrifices of past generations may account for the way that so many in the United States take so much for granted. Not having to fight for the rights and privileges made possible by freedom may well explain why so few understand just how precious and rare they truly are.

Perhaps the fact that young people of the past few generations have been given so much without having to earn it on their own has something to do with the problems so frequently highlighted by those who claim that American culture has been on a downward spiral for several decades. There is no need to list here all the evidence and statistics so often cited. The headlines of our daily newspapers offer them in bold print each morning whether we ask for them or not. It is a fair question, however, whether or not many of the problems plaguing American society can be traced to the fact that many individuals have lost the sense of unity and direction that so characterized the lives of our founding fathers and the succeeding generations who fought and sacrificed to protect their original dream. Lacking a clear vision of what the future can hold and the passion necessary to fulfill it, there is little wonder that many Americans have seemingly begun to question the meaningfulness of life without a challenge beyond that of chasing wealth.

When considering these issues it is interesting to think back to the motion picture "Rocky," and its many sequels. Written by Sylvester Stallone, the movie originally released in 1976 had a tremendous impact on a generation that not long before had experienced the many troubling circumstances surrounding the Vietnam War. The story involves a washed-up Philadelphia boxer, Rocky Balboa, who was, for all intents and purposes, a "nobody." With no real opportunities to prove himself, Rocky simply drifted through life, taking an occasional fight now and then to earn a few dollars and "stay in the game." As fate would have it, the heavyweight champion of the world, Apollo Creed, was looking for just such a man to take part in a marketing scheme in which the world champion, with no serious contenders, would give an unknown fighter a shot at the title.

Rising valiantly to the occasion, Rocky pushed himself to the limit in order to get in shape for the fight of his life. Through hard work and determination, coached all the way by his trainer, Mickey, Rocky arrived at the fight ready to change the world. As the story continues over various sequels, Rocky eventually beats the odds and becomes the new heavyweight champion of the world. Having reached his goal, Rocky then falls into the trap that so often ensnares champions. He begins to take life easy, believing himself immune to defeat. Forgetting the training regimen and discipline that allowed him to achieve greatness, Rocky eventually loses his title and is forced to once again look deep inside to discover whether or not the heart of a true champion beats within his chest.

To at least some degree this plot might be an apt metaphor for many of the problems associated with life in America today. Possessing a history throughout which disciplined individuals overcame great odds to achieve previously unimaginable success, many suggest that Americans today seem to lack any great unifying challenge. An unrivaled "superpower," one might argue that Americans, like Rocky, have for too long taken success for granted and have begun to grow "fat, dumb and happy." This may, in some measure, account for the way that attempts by such men as William J. Bennett, in his "Book of Virtues" and related publications, to remind Americans of the importance of morality and time-honored values are so often met with cynicism and even scorn. The thought that unrivaled success eventually leads to apathy may not be too far off the mark.

Whether or not the United States was actually experiencing a period of moral decline and was characterized by apathy and a lack of passion prior to September 11, 2001, there is no denying that the events of that Tuesday morning served to rouse the nation like nothing has since Pearl Harbor. The question of where this new-found patriotism and unity will carry the nation and how long the momentum will last is open to debate. The thought that continued adversity in the form of the ever-increasing acts of terrorism common in SPAR warfare might eventually lead America to reach new heights of unity and passion for the future may represent an unparalleled opportunity for a new generation of Americans to achieve a new level of greatness. Should Americans together with their allies emerge victorious from the trials of a "new world war," who is to say what a new generation tested in the fires of tribulation may accomplish. Though the future is by no means certain, there may never have been a people on earth more capable of meeting such a challenge than the citizens of the United States of America.

Epilogue

O n what must have been a brisk morning in early
October of 732 AD, they stood nervously beside the
Loire River in what is today southern France. Foot soldiers
armed with swords, shields, axes, and various other crude
implements of war watched and waited for the feared Muslim
horsemen who had brutally conquered Spain and laid waste to
much of southern Gaul. Led by Charles Martel, the Franks
could but wonder what carnage the day would bring.

The advancing Muslim army had crossed the Pyrenees
mountains some years before, and by all accounts had
enjoyed great success in the destruction of towns and the pil-
laging of palaces and homes as they slowly continued
northward. Their brutal reputation for burning churches and
slaying noblemen preceded them as they made their way to
the banks of the Loire. Under the capable direction of
Abderrahman, the Muslim warriors had every reason to
anticipate another glorious victory over the men of
Christendom, and to believe that by nightfall they would

once again be in a position to enjoy the spoils of war.

Since the death of Muhammad exactly one hundred years earlier, Islam had spread westward from the Arabian Peninsula to Egypt, swept across the remainder of North Africa, and had crossed the Straits of Gibraltar to gain a solid foothold in Spain. As Muslim armies advanced by both peaceful means and by the sword, it seemed inevitable that they would continue their northward march, eventually conquering all of Western Europe.

The exact details of what took place during the fierce battles fought in early October, 732, beside the Loire River have been lost to history. It is clear, however, that against all odds Charles Martel and his army of foot soldiers emerged victorious and the badly beaten Muslim horsemen retreated southward, never again to attempt an invasion north of the Pyrenees.

With their victory, at what has become known as the Battle of Tours, Charles Martel and his men were credited with stopping the northward advancement of Islam, and, thus, of saving Western Europe from unimaginable destruction. It is, perhaps, of interest to note that the grandson of Charles Martel, a man by the name of Charlemagne, was crowned Holy Roman Emperor on Christmas day in the year 800 AD. One wonders how world history would have been written had Martel and his soldiers not met the awesome challenge confronting them on that fateful autumn morning almost seven decades earlier.

At the dawn of the 21st century, as Muslim warriors once again set their sights on conquering western civilization, one wonders how present-day men of valor will respond. Some

1270 years after the Battle of Tours, will yet another Charles Martel emerge to defend the West from defeat at the hands of militant Muslims, or has the world grown far too complex for matters to be decided in such a manner?

Throughout this work, the argument has been presented that western civilization has been targeted for destruction by militant Muslims who would replace it with their own vision of an enlightened society. The reality that the forces working toward these ends now enjoy many real advantages over the West has inspired confidence that what began as a dream may be realized sooner than the original planners had anticipated.

The question of how the West will respond to this present-day threat depends in large measure on whether or not the threat itself will be recognized in time for an effective defense to be implemented. Had Charles Martel chosen to ignore the warnings that an awesome enemy would soon be approaching, the Battle of Tours would certainly have ended differently. Considering these issues, one wonders how people of the future will judge the actions of those involved in this struggle for world dominance. Will the preoccupation with partisan politics and economic supremacy blind the western world to issues of far greater importance? Will the insatiable demand for ever-expanding rights for the individual at the expense of the common good render democracy one of many failed attempts to govern mankind over the ages? Will the inability to adapt to new challenges render the leaders of western civilization powerless to combat a novel approach to waging war? The question of whether future historians will busy themselves writing the epitaph of western civilization or the account of how its people united to defeat an awesome enemy remains to be answered.

As the future continues to unfold, one thing is certain. The courage and ingenuity of today's leaders will be called upon and tested to an extent that has been unknown for many years. How the citizens of western nations respond to this challenge will determine whether our children and grandchildren continue to enjoy the liberty offered by democracy, or will be governed by men who claim the very mandate of Heaven.